THE ARBITRATION OF RIGHTS DISPUTES
IN THE PUBLIC SECTOR

THE ARBITRATION OF RIGHTS DISPUTES IN THE PUBLIC SECTOR

CLARENCE R. DEITSCH
and
DAVID A. DILTS

QUORUM BOOKS
New York • Westport, Connecticut • London

Library of Congress Cataloging-in-Publication Data

Deitsch, Clarence R.
    The arbitration of rights disputes in the public sector / Clarence
R. Deitsch and David A. Dilts.
        p.   cm.
    Includes bibliographical references.
    ISBN 0–89930–415–X (alk. paper)
    1. Employee-management relations in government—Law and
legislation—United States.   2. Grievance arbitration—United
States.   I. Dilts, David A.   II. Title.
KF5365.D45   1990
342.73′0684—dc20
[347.302684]   90–30016

British Library Cataloguing in Publication Data is available.

Library of Congress Catalog Card Number: 90–30016
ISBN: 0–89930–415–X

First published in 1990

Quorum Books, 88 Post Road West, Westport, CT   06881
An imprint of Greenwood Publishing Group, Inc.

Printed in the United States of America

♾™

The paper used in this book complies with the
Permanent Paper Standard issued by the National
Information Standards Organization (Z39.48–1984).

10 9 8 7 6 5 4 3 2 1

Contents

Preface

This book will provide labor relations practitioners with a basic guide for the arbitration of grievances in public employment. The focus is on ideas that will be the most useful to the agency official or union steward whose responsibility it is to represent their constituents in the grievance-arbitration procedure effectively. Although written primarily for practitioners working in state and local governments, this book is equally appropriate for individuals working in the federal or private sectors.

The book is organized into nine chapters and five appendices. Chapter 1 introduces the public sector and the labor relations systems found therein. Chapter 2 reviews various state bargaining statutes governing the arbitration of grievance disputes and teacher due-process hearings. Chapter 3 takes a brief look at the grievance process as a prelude to arbitration. Chapter 4 examines the institution of arbitration, focusing primarily upon the administrative agencies, the arbitrators, and the legal environment within which labor relations advocates must effectively discharge their representational duties. Chapter 5 treats procedural and evidential issues common to arbitration. Chapter 6 addresses contract interpretation issues while Chapter 7 focuses on the arbitration of discharge and disciplinary matters. Chapter 8 examines the decision making of neutrals and what can or cannot reasonably be expected of arbitrators. Chapter 9 summarizes the preceding chapters and makes the case for rights arbitration as the preferred method of dispute resolution.

The appendices contain information that is neither frequently found in "cookbook" summaries of the grievance-arbitration process nor available from a single source. Since the goal of the book is to equip the practitioner adequately and to represent his or her respective constituents effectively in the private system of industrial jurisprudence, this information is indispensable. Appendix 2 is the Code of Professional Responsibility for Arbitrators of Labor-Management Disputes. Appendix 3 contains the rules of the American Arbitration Association and the procedures of the Federal Mediation and Conciliation Service. Appendices 1, 4, and 5 contain sample arbitration awards issued in real-life cases. The "Annotated Bibliography" includes citations that were selected for their usefulness to both labor and management.

The authors are professional arbitrators. There has been no attempt to highlight the pluses or to gloss over the blemishes of the arbitration process. Instead, the authors attempt to "tell it as it is." However, the volume will inevitably reflect the value judgments of its authors as well as their professional training, expertise, and experience—hopefully, more of the latter than the former.

Collective Bargaining and Employer-Employee Relations in the Public Sector

This chapter introduces the public sector and the various systems of labor-management relations found therein. It forms the foundation and frame of reference for the material that follows, particularly for the discussion of the legal environment contained in Chapter 4.

THE PUBLIC SECTOR

The public sector comprises three levels of government: federal, state, and local. Labor-management relations in the federal sector are governed by the 1978 Civil Service Reform Act. At the state and local levels, there is no similar unifying statute or body of labor law; diversity is the rule. This differentiates the state and local legal environments from those of both the federal and the private sectors. To date, little has been written to assist practitioners and students with the diversity of rules and regulations governing public sector collective bargaining at the state and local levels. This chapter attempts to do just that—fill a serious gap in the literature concerning public sector collective bargaining at state and local levels.

Governmental units provide an extremely wide range of services at the state and local levels. Education, fire and police protection, and road maintenance do not even begin to scratch the surface as far as the very large number of services provided by these levels of government. It should not, therefore, be surprising that one specific government (e.g., one city) may bargain with a number of different unions. In this regard, collective bargaining at the state and local levels is certainly unique.

The uniqueness of state and local governments is not due solely to the large number of bargaining units; it can be traced to several other more substantive factors. In most cases, there are no substitute sources for public service. For example, even though there may be private schools within a specific governmental jurisdiction, private education may not be a viable substitute for the public education system for many families. Many of these governmental services are deemed essential to public health and safety. As such, their denial is viewed as harmful to the general public: a threat to health, safety, or property. Without police and fire protection, for example, a community is at risk. It is this potential harm to people and property, due to the lack of substitute service sources that is frequently cited for the characteristic prohibition of strikes by employees in the public sector.

The nature of a public good also contributes to the uniqueness of public sector collective bargaining. For most public goods, like national defense, for example, it is impossible to limit the benefits to those persons who have paid for the good. Stated somewhat differently, it is impossible to exclude those who have not paid for the good from the benefits of the good. Since this is the case, all are taxed to pay for services rendered by the government. Consequently, freedom of economic choice does not exist as it does in the private sector. Not only is the governmental unit the sole provider of the good or service, but, unlike the private sector sole provider, the monopolist, it can also compel the individual to pay for the good or service regardless of whether he or she wants that good or service.

The foregoing element of compulsion also distinguishes public sector exchange from its private sector counterpart. In private market exchange, payment must be rendered at the time the good or service is received. This permits the consumer to judge the value of the good or service in question and ultimately determine whether or not and how much of the good or service will be purchased and ultimately produced. The proximity of payment and receipt in private exchange, therefore, serves to promote efficiency by restraining the provider as far as the price charged.

In the public sector, on the other hand, the separation of payment and receipt coupled with the governmental unit's power to tax removes any similar restraints or incentives to be efficient. The only check on public sector management or incentive to be efficient is the public's unwillingness to pay taxes. Although much has been written and said about taxpayer resistance to public goods and services, it is much more difficult to mobilize and focus than consumer resistance in the marketplace, where displeasure can be registered by a simple refusal to buy. For this reason, when it comes to collective bargaining and the resultant increased labor costs due thereto, it is normal operating procedure for governmental units to prohibit the negotiation of wages. Wages and certain other terms and conditions of employment are not mandatory topics for collective bargaining in the federal sector. Negotiations in the private sector are not subject to similar legal restrictions.

The efficiency argument for prohibiting collective bargaining altogether in the public sector or, at minimum, severely limiting its scope is often couched in terms of sovereignty. This philosophical argument against collective bargaining in the public sector holds that, since government is the designated caretaker of sovereignty, the supreme decision-making authority through which the state is governed, the source of which is the people governed, it "cannot be given to, taken by, or shared with anyone."[1] Accordingly, the sovereignty argument mandates unilateral governmental determination of the terms and conditions of employment, that is, it prohibits joint employee-employer decision making. Employees, on the other hand, argue that reason warrants a limitation of sovereignty when and where justified by the public interest, as so often is the case where terms and conditions of employment are concerned. The sovereignty doctrine has been institutionalized through constitutional and statutory bars and restrictions upon public sector bargaining.

Whatever the inherent and relative merits of the various arguments, the foregoing factors have combined—to a greater or lesser extent depending upon the political jurisdiction under scrutiny—to shape the legal landscape of public sector collective bargaining, a landscape characterized by diversity rather than tedious uniformity.

LABOR-MANAGEMENT RELATIONS SYSTEMS

A number of different systems of labor-management relations have evolved in the public sector. These can be grouped into three broad categories: collective bargaining systems, meet-and-confer systems, and unilateral decision-making systems. The legal evolutionary chain responsible for each broad category is anything but clear. In some cases, collective bargaining may be the product of state statute, local ordinance, attorney general opinion, or state court decisions. In other cases, it develops spontaneously in de facto fashion. In Virginia, for example, collective bargaining evolved over a number of years. Virginia's experience with de facto collective bargaining, however, demonstrates an important aspect or feature of de facto systems:

[I]n May 1976 the Virginia Governor directed the Attorney General to challenge the [de facto] public sector bargaining relationships. Arlington County was chosen as the test jurisdiction because it contained examples of some of the different forms public employee unionization could take, and it was believed that a successful court challenge in that jurisdiction would provide a basis for nullifying bargaining of employee groups in all other jurisdictions. In *Commonwealth v. Bd. of Supervisors of Arlington County*, the state circuit court ruled that authority for the agreements was implied from the legislature's delegation of power to local governments to perform necessary services. However, the lower court's decision was appealed to the Virginia State Supreme Court which ruled in 1977 that without state legislation authorizing public sector collective bargaining all agreements were null and void. The level of local union representation in Virginia plummeted from 13 percent in 1976 to less than 1 percent by 1982.[2]

In short, without statutory protection, de facto bargaining systems can be easily abolished. These and related topics are treated at greater length in the next chapter.

The three systems of labor-management relations not only differ substantively from one another, but also differ significantly in terms of their impact upon the grievance arbitration process. Each system is examined below.

Collective Bargaining

Collective bargaining is a system of labor-management relations under which labor and management mutually determine the terms and conditions of employment. It is a system wherein employees and their employers jointly resolve the problems of the work place. Three phases make up the collective bargaining process: labor force organization, contract negotiation, and contract administration. Stated differently, there must be an organization before an agreement can be negotiated, and there must be an agreement before it can be administered. Organization occurs when a union succeeds in convincing a majority of the employees of the need for group action. Upon proof of such majority support, such as victory in a secret ballot election, some state or local agency will certify the union as the exclusive bargaining agent. In the private sector, this government agency is the National Labor Relations Board (NLRB). Contract negotiation may commence at this point.

Contract negotiation is that phase of collective bargaining wherein the representatives of the employees and employers meet, exchange information, argue, discuss, formulate, and agree to the rules and regulations that will govern their relationship during the course of the next several years. This private contract law covers a wide range of issues from compensation to work rules. It is through this negotiation process that employees and the union acquire rights in their dealings with management. Accepted labor relations dogma, the management reserved rights doctrine, holds that management retains all rights and privileges not wrested from its grasp and set to contract language during the negotiation process. In other words, a "Genesis" theory of management rights has evolved: "In the beginning, there was management, and employees possess only those rights that negotiation and statute have bestowed upon them."

Equally important, if not more so, than contract negotiation is contract administration. As in the case of public law, private contract law is not self-interpreting, self-enforcing, or self-administering. Once rights and privileges have been achieved through negotiation, they must be protected for however long the contract remains in force. This is accomplished through contract administration. The proximate mechanism of contract administration is the grievance-arbitration procedure, the vehicle through which rules and regulations embodied in a labor agreement are interpreted and enforced as the contract is applied and administered by management and the union in the day to day operation of the agency. In short, the grievance structure provides due process for the protection of the contractual rights of employees. Since contract administration may give a specific contract clause or provision an entirely different meaning from the one intended by its authors during negotiation, it is arguably the most important phase of collective bargaining and the focus of this book.

The driving mechanism of the bargaining process is bargaining power. According to Chamberlain and Kuhn, bargaining power is "the ability to secure another's agreement on one's own terms."[3] Expanding this definition and viewing it from a slightly different perspective, bargaining power is nothing more than the willingness of an opponent to agree to a party's proposal based upon a comparison of the benefits and costs of doing so. The heart of the negotiation process, then, consists of each party's attempt, through a variety of different tactics and strategies, to increase the other party's perceived benefits and to reduce the other party's perceived costs of agreeing to each proposal brought to the bargaining table for consideration. To the extent that a party is successful, bargaining power increases as does the likelihood of a favorable settlement.

A criticism often leveled against collective bargaining is that it is an adversary-based system of labor-management relations. This is admittedly the case. Before becoming too critical, however, remember that collective bargaining is a simple extension of the market system where all exchange takes place within a competitive and adversarial environment. As such, collective bargaining is no more adversarial in nature than other exchanges that occur within the competitive framework of free markets.[4] The same can be said regarding our legal and social systems. Competition and conflict characterize the political system, the judicial system, and modern professional sports. Very few institutions within the United States have escaped the pervasive influence of conflict. As long as competition provides the checks and balances necessary to prevent either labor or management from unilaterally imposing its will upon the other, collective bargaining dovetails nicely with other American economic, social, political, and cultural institutions. Indeed, to paraphrase H. Rap Brown's once highly controversial statement: "Collective bargaining is as American as cherry pie."[5]

Currently, thirty-five states have enacted statutes protecting the collective bargaining rights of one or more categories of public employees.[6] Consequently, it is not stretching the truth to conclude that collective bargaining is the most widely adopted system of labor-management relations in state and local government.

Meet-and-Confer Systems

Meet-and-confer systems of labor-management relations are relatively rare in state and local government simply because such systems do not provide employees a determinative impact upon conditions in the work place. Since meet-and-confer statutes do not mandate bargaining, they do not provide for exclusive bargaining representatives. Such legislation simply requires the unit of government to give its employees the opportunity to voice their concerns or to present their positions regarding employment-related issues. In this regard, employees have no more input than the general public regarding these issues. Only three states—Alabama, Georgia, and Missouri—rely exclusively upon meet-and-confer labor-management relations systems. Four other states—Indiana, Kansas, Nebraska, and Texas—have meet-and-confer statutes for specific groups of employees— the first two for state employees and the last two for teachers.

The effectiveness of meet-and-confer systems depends upon the benevolence of agency managers. When they are concerned with employee welfare, solicit employee input, and implement employee suggestions, meet-and-confer systems can work. All too often, however, such systems are almost totally pro forma and without substance unless employees can bring political pressure to bear upon agency and department through appeals to the voting public.

Unilateral Decision-making Systems

Twelve states have neither collective bargaining nor meet-and-confer statutes. Two of these, however, do have widespread de facto bargaining, and another has an attorney general's opinion that permits collective bargaining—leaving eight states totally without the form or substance of bilateral decision-making. None of these states are industrial states, and all are "right-to-work" law states.

Unilateral decision making by management needs little explanation. Simply put, management has the exclusive right to set and enforce whatever terms and conditions of employment it deems appropriate, limited by specific regulatory statute and constitutional provision only.

Labor-Management Relations Systems, Employee Rights, and Grievances

The system of industrial labor-management relations that evolves within or is adopted by a unit of government has a significant impact upon employee rights and, therefore, upon employee grievances. An effectively functioning mechanism for the resolution of grievances is a prerequisite for good management. Witness the establishment of such procedures by nonunionized firms in the private sector because "it is good personnel practice and policy."[7] In a few cases these procedures go so far as to provide for binding arbitration of unresolved grievance disputes.

Since nonunion grievance procedures are of relatively recent origin and, consequently, untested, little evidence exists as to whether they provide employees a determinative say in decision making or guarantee employee rights. Reason, however, would seem to indicate that unilaterally established procedures are not as effective as jointly established ones. The explanation is simple: employee interests are better served through independent representation at the time of grievance procedure creation and administration than through convenience to management.

Indiana is an excellent case in point. Under the State Personnel Act, employees have the right to file and appeal grievances to the State Personnel Commission. If the commission rules in favor of the employee but fails to provide the remedy requested, the employee has the right to appeal the disputed remedy to arbitration. On the other hand, if the commission rules against the employee, there is no further avenue of appeal for either grievance or remedy. In other words, arbitration is available to an employee only when the state admits wrongdoing—hardly an independent and neutral forum for the resolution of grievances and protection of employee rights, and hardly a system that guarantees due process.[8]

By the same token, the benefits of grievance-arbitration procedures fashioned and administered within the framework of collective bargaining are well documented.[9] Here, two autonomous organizations—the union and management—police and enforce the contract to protect their respective interests.

CONCLUSION

Public sector collective bargaining is a highly controversial topic because of the unique characteristics of public sector firms, most notably the nature of the goods and services provided and the manner in which these goods and services are financed. These essential goods and services have few close substitutes. Interruption in the flow of these goods and services due to a work stoppage, for example, would impose serious hardship among the consuming public. As for financing, these goods and services are provided through the government's ability to tax. This guaranteed revenue source eliminates economic freedom of choice and, with it, the major incentive for the public sector firm or agency to be efficient and competitive. Collective bargaining in the public sector has been opposed on both grounds.

Three types of industrial relations systems characterize the public sector landscape: collective bargaining systems, meet-and-confer systems, and unilateral decision-making systems. Only eight states have completely shunned bilateral input in some form, choosing instead to remain with unilateral decision making. The predominance of some form of bilateral decision making mirrors the documented benefits of such schemes, particularly with regard to employee due process under a variety of different grievance-arbitration procedures.

NOTES

1. Michael H. Moscow et al., *Collective Bargaining in Public Employment* (New York: Random House, 1970), p. 17.

2. Statement of AFSCME before Subcommittee on Labor of the Committee on Labor and Human Resources, U.S. Senate, 100th Cong., 2d sess., *Reviewing Practices and*

Operations under the National Labor Relations Act (Washington, D.C.: GPO, 1988), p. 148.

3. Neil W. Chamberlain and James W. Kuhn, *Collective Bargaining*, 2d ed. (New York: McGraw-Hill, 1965), p. 170.

4. For a further discussion, see: David A. Dilts and Clarence R. Deitsch, *Labor Relations* (New York: Macmillan, 1983), pp. 5–7.

5. Alphonso Pinkney, *American Way of Violence* (New York: Random House, 1972).

6. AFSCME Research Department reported in the Senate Subcommittee hearings cited in note 2, pp. 151–64.

7. Richard B. Freeman, "Contraction and Expansion: The Divergence of Private Sector and Public Sector Unionism in the United States," *Journal of Economic Perspectives* (Spring 1988), 2:63–68.

8. David A Dilts and Clarence R. Deitsch, "Arbitration Lost: The Public Sector Assault on Arbitration," *Labor Law Journal* (March 1984), 35:182–88.

9. For examples, see: Archibald Cox, "Rights under a Labor Agreement," *Harvard Law Review* (February 1956), 56:601–57; S. H. Slichter, J. J. Healy, and E. R. Livernash, *The Impact of Collective Bargaining on Management* (Washington, D.C: Brookings Institution, 1960), Chapters 23–26; and D. A. Dilts and C. R. Deitsch, *Labor Relations*, Chapter 11.

2

Grievances: Causes, Effects, and Proper Handling

Grievances are the inevitable by-product of every employment relationship. Whenever two or more individuals interact on a regular basis, there is the potential for friction and conflict. This is particularly true in work environments where employees and managers have different goals and objectives. Conflict is not necessarily bad for the relationship; when properly managed, it can be a catalyst for growth and development.[1] Grievances identify problems in the work place, with work rules, contract language, and the implementation of these rules and contract language. In doing so, they provide the information on which solutions may be based. By the same token, unchecked conflict can destroy the employment relationship and irreparably injure both parties. The challenge, therefore, is to properly manage conflict, first diagnosing the problem and then treating it. In this regard, grievances serve as the pulse of the employment relationship, indicating its overall health.

THE NEED FOR GRIEVANCE ARBITRATION

There must be some way of resolving grievances arising in the day-to-day employment relationship. Two methods immediately come to mind: economic warfare (turnover, termination, strike, lockout—"the law of tooth and fang") and court litigation. Unfortunately, both methods are extremely costly for both employee and employers, if not in explicit expenditure, then in morale and, ultimately, productivity. The parties, therefore, choose a more peaceful and less costly method of grievance dispute resolution.

At first glance, it may appear that many modern-day industrial relations systems—unilateral, meet-and-confer, and collective bargaining—have adopted the same approach for resolving grievance disputes: the creation and implementation of formal grievance procedures consisting of multiple steps where employees and their representatives meet and confer with the representatives of management in an attempt to resolve their differences. The similarity in approach among these industrial relations systems, however, ends here. Meet-and-confer and unilateral systems do not, for the most part, provide a final and binding resolution of grievance disputes by an outside, neutral third party should the dispute remain unresolved after passing through the "private" steps of the grievance procedure.[2] Instead, the final decision remains that of either a management representative or governing body, such as a state agency, school board, or city council.

The reason that meet-and-confer and unilateral systems do not provide for grievance arbitration is the same reason that the political jurisdictions that gave them their existence oppose collective bargaining, or bilateral decision making, in the first place, namely, the loss of control and sovereignty with regard to the issue in dispute. While such arrangements may function as a temporary safety valve for employee discontent, frustration, and emotion, they only serve to postpone the ultimate resolution of the dispute by means of economic warfare or court litigation.

In an employment relationship characterized by collective bargaining, on the other hand, where sovereignty and other arguments have already been overcome, there remain no philosophical or ideological obstacles to the final and binding resolution of grievance disputes through the decision of an outside, neutral third party. Consequently, labor agreements almost universally provide for the arbitration of unresolved grievances; that is, they cap the grievance procedure with arbitration. Hence, labor and management have not only agreed upon the rules and regulations that will govern their behavior toward one another during the term of the labor agreement, but they have also agreed as to how they will disagree and resolve disputes concerning the application and interpretation of these rules and regulations when they arise, that is, through the grievance-arbitration procedure.[3]

Without such an internal mechanism for the final and binding resolution of contract interpretation disputes, the contract would become meaningless and, along with it, the bargaining process that generated it. Constant recourse to either court litigation or to economic warfare would so burden the labor relations system as to make it unworkable. The grievance-arbitration process, therefore, is an excellent mechanism for channeling conflict to productive ends. It is as therapeutic as economic warfare, more therapeutic than court litigation, and less costly than either of these alternatives.

The therapeutic benefits of arbitration warrant further discussion. The benefits of physical exercise as a means for releasing tension, stress, and worry are well known. Arbitration serves much the same purpose within the labor-management relationship. It rivals strike activity and surpasses court litigation as a cathartic outlet for employee frustration, emotion, and discontent. As a less formal mechanism of dispute resolution, the parties can say things and introduce evidence that would not be tolerated within the formal structure of the court system. They can air their differences—"get things off their chests"—without regard to the procedural strictures of a court. Even though an arbitrator may rule against them, the parties have had the opportunity to "vent their spleens." Discontent vented, the parties may once again productively resume their duties. What makes this particularly attractive is that the cost of grievance arbitration, although significant, pales in comparison to economic warfare and court litigation.

Another factor recommending grievance arbitration is that the process generates a body of decisions, or shop-case law, that the parties may find useful for resolving future contract interpretation and application disputes. The high cost of court litigation makes it a less appealing option for resolution of contract disputes.

So effective have grievance-arbitration procedures been in channeling conflict to productive purposes that many nonunion employers in the private sector have emulated their unionized counterparts by making these procedures part of their personnel and human resources programs. Employers who have done so have realized an additional and, in some cases, unexpected benefit: reduced liability in wrongful discharge cases. Whereas an arbitrator's remedial power in such cases is limited to reinstatement with back pay, courts may range much further in fashioning remedies—oftentimes requiring the payment of punitive damages in addition to reinstatement with back pay.

With this overview of the grievance-arbitration procedure, we turn to a detailed examination of grievances and the reasons for the creation of the grievance-arbitration procedure. A full understanding of the nature of grievances and their causes is a prerequisite to their prevention, proper handling, and resolution, or rather, the channeling of conflict to productive ends.

GRIEVANCES DEFINED

Grievances, in common usage, are complaints. In the labor relations arena, however, the word is more specifically defined by the labor agreement or statute, typically, disputes involving the proper interpretation and/or application of the provisions of the labor agreement. Thus, while an employee may, for example, have a complaint about the way in which overtime is assigned, it is not a grievance as long as the overtime is assigned in accordance with the provisions of the labor agreement. Simply put, all grievances are complaints, but not all complaints are grievances.

Less frequently, grievances are broadly defined as any dispute that arises between the parties during the effective term of the labor agreement. With such broad language—language that makes grievance and complaint synonymous terms—disputes that the parties never intended to make eligible for in-house resolution often find their way into the grievance procedure. Witness the arbitration case that one of the authors was called upon to hear and decide: a domestic dispute between a husband (bargaining unit member and grievant) and wife (supervisor) concerning who would drive to work during bad weather. Unfortunately, the broad definition of grievance can and has been expanded to encompass such non–job-related controversies. The parties to the employment relationship, therefore, must adopt a definition of grievance that best meets their needs and services their relationship, taking care to exclude irrelevant issues that unduly burden the grievance resolution machinery.

GRIEVANCE CAUSES

All grievances are simultaneously different and alike. They are different with regard to personalities, contract language, past practice, or facts and circumstances involved in the dispute. They are alike in that the employee sees the filing of a grievance as promoting his or her self-interest in some way. Should the complaint lack contractual merit and, therefore, not warrant a remedy, the benefit achieved may be nothing more than the satisfaction of venting frustration.

Grievances can be classified by cause and, accordingly, by the type of employee interest served by their filing. These categories are: grievances caused by misunderstandings, grievances caused by intentional contract violations, and symptomatic grievances, which are caused by problems outside the scope of the contract.

Misunderstandings

Misunderstandings are possible whenever people communicate by the spoken or written word. The labor agreement is the written record of what labor and management verbally agreed to during contract negotiations and embodies the possibility of both sources of misunderstanding; the parties may fail to precisely verbalize what each believes was agreed to and then compound matters by committing still another interpretation to writing. Even if the parties precisely verbalize their agreement and commit it to writing, unforeseen circumstances will often arise requiring the specific application of theretofore clear and undisputed contract language. The parties can hardly be expected to anticipate such circumstances and make specific contractual provisions for them. Hence, there always exists the potential for disagreement and dispute stemming from misunderstandings.

Misunderstandings as causes of grievances can be traced to three broad sources: disputed facts surrounding the application of specific contract provisions, unclear contract provisions, and ignorance of contract provisions. The best example of the first category is the case of an employee disciplined for the infraction of work rules. The discipline may be challenged on the basis of whether the employee actually did what he or she is charged with, whether the discipline was reasonable in light of attendant circumstances, and whether proper procedures were followed when the discipline was assessed. Consistency of treatment of rules violators also generates honest disagreements between the parties as the labor agreement is administered and enforced.

The single greatest source of misunderstandings-based grievances may be unclear contract language traceable to the negotiators' unwillingness to confront and resolve difficult issues, choosing instead to shirk responsibility by hiding behind purposely vague contract phrases; the negotiators' inability to precisely communicate what has been agreed to; or the negotiators' failure to carefully proofread the labor agreement they have committed to writing. The case of the missing comma illustrates the last point; problems are caused by inadequate attention to detail. This now classic contract provision provided for the promotion of "the senior most qualified employee." The union read this phrase to mean the promotion of "the senior most, qualified employee," while the management read it to mean the promotion of "the senior, most qualified employee." In the absence of the proper placement of the comma, each meaning is equally plausible. No doubt the parties were satisfied with the bargain struck concerning the issue during contract negotiations, but they omitted the comma, thereby creating problems for those charged with administering and enforcing this provision for the duration of the labor agreement. Proofreading and testing the language of each paragraph of each article is essential to assure that the language clearly and precisely conveys the bargain the parties struck and to avoid resultant grievances.

The final source of misunderstandings is contract ignorance. While inexcusable for both union members and supervisors, a supervisor's lack of familiarity with contract provisions is more understandable. Supervisors are rewarded for attaining production and service goals, not for knowing and enforcing contracts. The link between effective grievance management and the achievement of production and service goals all too often has not been pointed out to supervisors and is not well understood by them. Under these circumstances, it should not be surprising that supervisors' actions often spawn grievances.

Regardless of the source of misunderstanding—be it disputed facts surrounding the application of specific contract provisions, unclear contract provisions, or contract ignorance—there remains one constant throughout: employees use the grievance procedure to protect contractual rights, or what they perceive to be contractual rights.

Intentional Contract Violations

The parties to a collective bargaining relationship are subject to two internal sets of rules and regulations, namely, the labor contract and past practice; the latter is often referred to as "shop-common law." Past practice consists of the ways in which the parties have mutually resolved problems, handled issues, and rendered decisions in the day-to-day operation of the firm or agency. In a real sense, past practice is an implied contract every bit as binding as an explicitly written contract. Indeed, past practice can serve to amend the contract where the latter is silent, vague, or, less frequently, clear.

Past practice inconsistent with contract language typically provides the backdrop for intentional contract violations that produce grievances. Most often, management is the transgressor because management has more opportunities for intentional violations as active administrator of the labor agreement. Management is also more likely to have ideological problems with the limits placed upon its decision-making power by the provisions of the labor agreement. In short, management has greater opportunity and motive to violate the labor agreement and, hence, will be more disposed to use an emergent practice to free itself from contractual obligations than will the union whenever it is convinced they are not in the best interests of the general public or agency.

This is not to say that the union will not capitalize on a favorable practice should the opportunity arise. There is, however, a major difference between the union's behavior and that of management. Since the union acquires its rights and privileges through contract provisions, it will attempt to leverage a favorable practice toward expanded employer obligations embodied in a specific contract provision. Take the case where management permitted street maintenance employees a ten-minute clean-up period despite contract language limiting such a period to five minutes. When management subsequently attempted to return to a literal enforcement of the contract provision, the union resisted and filed a grievance. To management's chagrin, the arbitrator ruled that established practice had the force of law and served to amend the labor agreement.

Although grievances stemming from intentional contract violations arise less frequently than those stemming from misunderstandings, there will always be some manager, union official, or union member who will try to obtain some privilege not permitted or conveyed by the labor agreement. Both parties, therefore, must be ever vigilant for any practice contrary to the language and spirit of the labor agreement that might provide aggressive individuals the opportunity to challenge negotiated rights, or they risk losing them.

Symptomatic Grievances

The final category of grievances is symptomatic grievances, the hardest to identify and prevent. As the name implies, the grievance itself is not the real problem. Instead, the grievance mirrors job- or non–job-related problems—problems that produce on-the-job behavior that leads to discipline and attendant grievances or, simply, the filing of trivial grievances because of frustration. There are three causes of symptomatic grievances: personal problems, union politics, and unfavorable contract language.

Personal problems affect an employee's outlook and attitude. For example, an employee suffering from an unhappy marriage, other domestic problems, or substance abuse may vent frustration by aggressive or hostile behavior that leads to the filing of grievances. Take the case of the young schoolteacher who had a normally congenial and cooperative attitude but suddenly became withdrawn. Her colleagues had noticed that for several days she had avoided personal contact and was very abrupt with almost everyone, even her closest friends. Her department chairperson asked her if there was a problem with which he or anyone else could provide assistance. The teacher filed a sexual harassment charge and grievance alleging unwarranted sexual attention. During a routine investigation of the grievance, the union representative found that the teacher had some sort of personal problem but could not identify the specifics. The teacher's sexual harassment charge had been processed to the superintendent and the grievance certified for arbitration before the union representative identified the problem: the teacher's fiancé had been diagnosed with terminal lung cancer and died the day after the fourth-step grievance meeting. At this juncture, all the sad circumstances surrounding her actions became known. The grievance and charge were dropped and the grievant received much-needed assistance and support from both management and the union. Unfortunately, however, personal problems of this nature will all too often go undetected and untreated, unnecessarily burdening both the employee and the grievance procedure.

Drug and alcohol abuse are particularly thorny problems. Substance abuse produces grievances in two ways: discipline for irrational behavior caused by intoxication and for absenteeism. Unfortunately, discipline is not well suited to remedying substance abuse. Consequently, unions and employers have increasingly turned to programs outside the traditional grievance framework to tackle this cause of symptomatic grievances. It is important to note, however, that there often comes a point when, if other remedies fail, discipline and discharge may be the only methods of ridding the agency of the devastating impact of substance abuse.

Lack of self-actualization frequently produces grievances. Such problems stem either from not using the skills and talents of an employee fully or from requiring an employee to perform some job-related task that he or she has not been trained to do. In either case, the result is employee frustration and, ultimately, grievances.

Take the case of the cook at a major state-run hospital in the Midwest. Early in her employment, she was a model employee, congenial and efficient. Several months later, however, she became withdrawn, sullen, uncooperative, and the quality of her work declined noticeably. She also began to file trivial grievances. Quite by accident, while investigating one of these grievances, the union representative discovered that she could not read. In her position as cook, she was required to read instructions on food preparation, safety, and equipment maintenance. When the cook she was to replace was present during her orientation period, the grievant's reading ability was never tested. When the previous cook retired and the grievant had to fend for herself, her sole guidance being written instructions, the work environment suddenly became strange and threatening. She became insecure, ineffective, and frustrated, and she reacted by striking out at that environment by filing trivial grievances. Fortunately, in this case, the source of these symptomatic grievances was rather easily eliminated through additional instruction.

Local union governance is a highly political process. Elections almost invariably provide for the direct participation of all union members, making the local union much more democratic than the national union. Local union leadership is judged primarily by its handling of grievances. Winning a grievance wins votes; losing a grievance loses votes. Given the highly political nature of local union office and the fact that union officials are evaluated by rank-and-file union members on the basis of their handling of grievances, unsuccessful office seekers or would-be office holders sometimes embarrass successful candidates by filing unwinnable grievances in an attempt to improve their own chances of success in the next election.

Management should resist the temptation to support any political faction within the union, which merely spawns further predatory behavior on each faction's part—and more grievances. Instead, management must be sufficiently perceptive to see political grievances for what they are and steer a course consistent with contractual and statutory obligations.

Closely related to politically motivated grievances and intentional violations are those grievances designed to highlight unfavorable contract language. The union may have negotiated language that, in retrospect, is a bad bargain. To illustrate its dissatisfaction and to demonstrate a need for changes in the contract, the union may file grievances, even where clear contract language has been properly interpreted and applied. At best, the union hopes to amend the contract in much the same way it does through intentional contract violations. Failing in this regard, the union hopes to make the grievance the basis for renegotiating what is perceived to be unfavorable contract language. Again, the grievance is symptomatic of some other problem—dissatisfaction with a negotiated contract provision.

At first glance, symptomatic grievances may appear to be an inappropriate use of the grievance procedure, or even an abuse of that structure. However, because grievances serve as the pulse of the employment relationship, indicating its overall health, symptomatic grievances are useful; they generate important information regarding the well-being of individual employees. For example, problems of self-actualization and substance abuse, which transcend the individual employee and adversely affect agency productivity, may be first identified through symptomatic grievances. Care must be taken with symptomatic grievances, however. An effectively functioning grievance procedure is one that is sufficiently flexible to accommodate symptomatic grievances as well as true grievances, but not so flexible as to allow symptomatic grievances to overwhelm it, rendering it impotent to perform its primary task of resolving true grievances.

GRIEVANCE RESOLUTION PROCEDURES

Virtually all labor agreements contain a grievance procedure, generally a multistep process that provides an internal mechanism for resolving conflict. As discussed at the outset of this chapter, without a grievance procedure and the right to strike, the only forum left for resolving alleged contract violations is the court system. Litigation in the courts is expensive, time consuming, and can create political and morale problems. Therefore, the less intrusive and more peaceful internal process is the first choice of most employers, unions, and employees.

The typical grievance procedure involves three to four steps: the discovery of evidence, a chance to review and re-evaluate contract language and its application, and the opportunity for an employee to air disagreements in an informal and nonthreatening forum.

The discovery of evidence is critically important to the resolution of any conflict. Too often people will rely on their own perceptions and biases to form conclusions. The standard requirement that grievances be investigated and the evidence discovered be made available to both parties provides an objective basis for decision making within the grievance procedure. In fact, it is not uncommon for the union to withdraw or management to grant a grievance after a complete investigation has disclosed evidence that may not have been known when the action in question took place.

An orderly multistep framework for reviewing managerial decisions permits upper-level management to evaluate personnel, to ensure that the agency has its best people in sensitive decision-making positions. For example, a manager whose actions are persistently challenged through the grievance procedure may have a personality flaw that impedes his or her effectiveness in that particular position. Once identified through the grievance procedure, the flaw may be easily corrected or neutralized by the manager's transfer to another position. In short, the grievance procedure permits the agency to make effective use of its human resources. From the union's perspective, on the other hand, such a system builds trust and morale by guaranteeing due process—protection from arbitrary and capricious treatment.

The grievance procedure provides employees and managers with an informal process where they can air complaints and disagreements. The usual view of a grievance procedure is that management acts and the union reacts. There is considerable truth in this view; what is often missed, however, is that, once issues are brought into the procedure, management can also express dissatisfaction. Many labor contracts provide for the filing of grievances by management, and virtually all contracts provide for the resolution of disciplinary matters through the grievance procedure.

The informality and predictability of the grievance procedure are critical to its success. An employee may not be willing to register a complaint about something that is important to him or her if the complaint procedure is unduly formal, costly, or threatening. Knowing what comes next and that meritorious grievances are sustained and remedied and nonmeritorious ones do not foster employee confidence that justice will be served. This leads to routine use of the procedure and the benefits stemming therefrom, namely, increased morale and productivity. The benefits, however, will occur only if the procedure is properly structured.

STRUCTURE OF THE GRIEVANCE PROCEDURE

There is no single ideal structure for all grievance procedures. The ideal format will vary from one employment relationship to the next, depending upon the individual needs, personalities, characteristics, and circumstances of each relationship. However, all grievance procedures share the common characteristic of having multiple steps. In this regard, they are similar to the multitiered judicial system. The first step brings together lower-level officials in both the agency and the union, while the last step prior to arbitration normally requires the review of the highest-ranking official from the agency and his or her union counterpart. Probably the most common grievance procedure in the public sector contains three steps: the first requires discussions between the union steward and the first-level supervisor, the second requires discussions between the chief steward and the first-level supervisor's boss, and the third requires the personnel manager and the chairperson of the bargaining committee to meet and confer. As noted earlier, should this internal process fail to produce a mutually acceptable solution to the dispute, the vast majority of contracted statutes require arbitration for a final and binding resolution.

The contract normally specifies time limits for filing grievances, responses by management, and, if the grievant is still dissatisfied, appeals to the next step. Generally, an employee must file a grievance within thirty to sixty calendar days of the date of the incident giving rise to the grievance, or the date the grievant should have become aware of the incident. Management will then have seven to fourteen days in which to respond to the grievance. If the grievant is still dissatisfied, an appeal to the next step must be filed within seven to fourteen calendar days, and so on, until all internal steps have been exhausted. The grievant is then generally given from seven to thirty days in which to appeal the grievance to arbitration.

Time limits are provided to give the process predictability and to guarantee that grievances are processed in a timely manner. Should either party fail to abide by the time limits in filing or answering a grievance, arbitrators will generally rule against them for having procedurally violated the contract.[4] This, however, does not bar the parties from agreeing to extend time limits to guarantee a complete investigation of all facts and circumstances surrounding the dispute. Agreements to extend time limits, however, should always be committed to writing and signed to protect the interests of both parties.

Grievance provisions also commonly contain language defining narrowly or in broad terms, grievances, those eligible to file grievances (e.g., nonprobationary employees), and the specifics of the arbitration process, which will be discussed later in the book. By providing as much guidance as possible to the arbitrator through precise terminology, the parties reduce the chances of the arbitrary substitution of the judgment of an outsider for that of the parties, making the process more predictable and responsive to their needs. Less discretion is allowed the arbitrator to substitute his or her judgment for that of those most familiar with the industry, agency, and employment relationship, and the unique problems associated therewith, namely, labor and management. The parties retain a greater degree of control over substantive contract matters, relinquishing only what is necessary to resolve a specific dispute. In short, while it is always important to be as precise as possible in contract negotiation, it is particularly so with regard to the language of the grievance-arbitration procedure.

THE EFFECTIVE GRIEVANCE PROCEDURE

A properly structured grievance procedure will only function as well as those responsible for its administration will allow. There are two primary indicators of the health of the grievance process: the number of grievances filed and the step at which they are settled. Too few grievances may indicate that the employees have little faith in the process and those charged with its administration. Too many grievances may indicate that management, the union, or both are not fulfilling their obligations to bargain in good faith. Unfortunately, no single per capita grievance number indicates an effectively functioning process. While the extremes will indicate problems, even to the most casual observers, the parties will simply have to exercise good judgment in all other cases to detect problems with the grievance procedure.

Most grievances should be resolved during the early steps of the grievance process. It is here that the representatives most familiar with the facts and circumstances of the case have the opportunity to reach a settlement. If they do not, serious problems may exist. The most common of these are the union's failure to drop meritless grievances and first- or second-line management's unwillingness or lack of authority to resolve routine complaints. This reluctance to settle disputes early in the grievance procedure is due largely to politics on the part of both labor and management. As noted earlier, local union offices are highly political. Mindful of the possible vote loss that may accompany grievance denial, incumbent officials may pass the buck. Second-line managers may have a similar desire to avoid offending their colleagues—in this case, first-line managers. In both cases, the result is the same: grievances that are processed further along in the grievance procedure than warranted in their inherent merit due to a search for someone else to blame for an adverse decision. There is no reasonable explanation, on the other hand, for management's failure to delegate the authority necessary for early-stage grievance settlement. A good faith intention and the authority to resolve grievances at the earliest opportunity in the grievance structure are prerequisites for good labor-management relations.

Too few grievances processed to the final steps of the grievance may also indicate a problem—that one or the other side is caving in. This is most often due to preoccupied production-oriented managers who will concede almost anything to minimize the time they must devote to anything other than the pursuit of their immediate production or service goals. Acquiescence is less likely in the case of the union. If employees believe that they are not being properly represented, they will remove their representatives from office. In either case, this behavior undermines the bargaining relationship by preventing the parties from finding mutually beneficial solutions to their problems. Collective bargaining is based on the notion that bilateral decision making will better approximate the competitive result than unilateral decision making. If either management or the union fails to represent its constituents in good faith, the collective bargaining system will not function to the mutual benefit of all parties concerned—labor, management, and the public.

Other symptoms of a poorly functioning grievance procedure include absenteeism, high employee turnover, low productivity, litigation, and various job actions, all of which are correctable through a properly structured and administered grievance mechanism. Labor and management must carefully monitor the operation of the grievance procedure. Should problems occur, corrective action should be taken immediately.

CONCLUSION

Grievances are a part of all organizations, arising whenever individuals interact on a regular basis. The complexity and diversity of the modern organization, however, constitute a particularly fertile environment for the growth of conflict. Conflict is not necessarily bad for the relationship. When properly managed, it can promote growth and development. A properly structured and administered grievance procedure is a prerequisite for channeling conflict toward productive ends.

Proper structuring and administration of any dispute resolution mechanism requires an understanding of grievances and their causes. While all grievances are similar in that employees view the filing of a grievance as promoting their self-interest in some way, they differ with regard to personalities, contract language, past practice, or facts and circumstances involved in the dispute. However, grievances may be categorized by one of three causes: misunderstandings, intentional contract violations, or problems transcending the contract. The latter category, often called symptomatic grievances because the grievance itself is not the problem but simply symptomatic of job- or non–job-related problems, is the most difficult to detect, remedy, and prevent.

The specific format the grievance procedure takes will vary substantially from one employment relationship to the next, depending upon the individual needs, personalities, characteristics, and circumstances of each relationship. Most grievance procedures, however, consist of multiple steps—usually three to five—where progressively higher ranking labor and management officials meet in an attempt to resolve the dispute if it is not resolved in previous steps. Should the dispute remain unresolved after these "private" steps of the grievance procedure, most contracts require its submission to arbitration for final settlement.

There is no simple measure of how well the dispute resolution process functions. It must be closely monitored by both labor and management to detect problems when they first occur. Resources can then be directed toward their speedy solution.

NOTES

1. K. Thomas, "Conflict and Conflict Management," in *Handbook of Industrial and Organizational Psychology*, ed. M. D. Dunnette (Chicago: Rand McNally, 1976), pp. 889–936.

2. Clarence R. Deitsch and David A. Dilts, "Arbitration Challenged: The Case of Indiana," *Journal of Collective Negotiations in the Public Sector*, vol. 10(2), 1981, pp. 173–79; idem, "*Rockville Training Center v. Alvin Peschke et al.*: Vindication of Court Rationale Underlying the Steelworkers Trilogy," *Employee Relations Law Journal*, vol. 10(1), 1984, pp. 95–105.

3. For a more detailed discussion of the role of unions, see: Richard B. Freeman and James Medoff, *What Do Unions Do?* (New York: Basic Books, 1984), particularly Chapters 1–2.

4. For a further discussion of this topic, see the next chapter and Owen Fairweather, *Practice and Procedures in Labor Arbitration* (Washington, D.C.: Bureau of National Affairs, 1983), pp. 18 and 92.

3

Alternatives and Preliminaries to Arbitration

Arbitration is one of several methods commonly used in the United States to resolve industrial relations disputes. Others include mediation, litigation, and work stoppages.

MEDIATION

Mediation is the dispute resolution technique wherein a neutral assists the parties, primarily through the art of persuasion, to compromise and reach a workable voluntary agreement. Because mediation is inherently private in nature, remaining hidden from view when successful, its effectiveness as a dispute resolution technique is difficult to determine. Judging from its widespread acceptance and use by labor relations practitioners in both the public and private sectors, however, mediation's contribution to peaceful labor relations has been and remains significant. Indeed, it is the third-party dispute resolution technique most frequently used in both the public and private sectors for avoiding and settling contract negotiation disputes.[1]

LITIGATION

Litigation, another method of resolving disputes growing out of the employer-employee relationship, includes equity proceedings (orders directed toward an individual or group of individuals requiring a particular course of action or inaction) and suits to enforce contracts, statutes, and ordinances, as well as suits to recover damages. Litigation may proceed through the judicial system or through an administrative law agency. The latter are public agencies whose responsibilities are to administer, interpret, and enforce the provisions of those statutes that gave them their existence. The basic function of these independent, quasi-judicial administrative law agencies is "the execution of the legislature's general will in a multitude of particular instances, far too numerous for the courts to handle directly."[2] Examples of such agencies include the NLRB, the Kansas Public Employment Relations Board (PERB and other similar state agencies), the Equal Employment Opportunity Commission (EEOC), the Occupational Safety and Health Administration (OSHA), the Unemployment Security Division, and the Enforcement Division of the U.S. Department of Labor (FLSA). Whatever the path of litigation, it entails substantial explicit and implicit costs. Not only does it involve the expenditure of large sums of money for legal fees and other litigious accouterments, like court reporters, but it is also a very time-consuming process—time during which the dispute is left to fester, further increasing frustration and decreasing employee morale with the consequent adverse impact upon productivity.

WORK STOPPAGES

Labor relations disputes not resolved through mediation or litigations are often resolved through work stoppages (i.e., strikes and lockouts). Included in this category are the many job actions that stop short of a complete work stoppage: rolling sickouts, "blue flu," chalk dust influenza, refusal to perform nonessential duties, work-to-rule, and the like. The United States experiences far fewer work stoppages than most developed countries around the world. Since passage of the National Labor Relations Act (NLRA) in 1935, less than one quarter of one percent of total available worker hours has been lost to industrial work stoppages; the comparable figure for European countries exceeds one percent. Despite this exemplary record of industrial peace, the disputes that do occur make news and often create inconvenience for the public and hardships for workers, unions, and employers alike.

Although several states (e.g., Montana, Ohio, Michigan, and Illinois) permit limited use of strikes by specific groups of public employees, most states, as well as the federal government, have prohibited its use by their employees. This prohibition, however, creates another problem: where employees are denied the ability to impose costs upon an employer, as the right to strike, they are also denied the right to bargain substantively. Stated somewhat differently, if there are no costs associated with the failure to reach an agreement, employers will have little reason to avoid failure, that is, to come to terms. The demands of employees simply would not be taken seriously; there would not be any incentive to bargain in good faith. In short, employees would not possess any bargaining power.

TYPES OF ARBITRATION

As a result of the prohibition of strikes in the public sector, an alternative method for resolving contract negotiation disputes has evolved. This substitute for strike activity is *interest arbitration*—the procedure wherein the parties submit a dispute involving the creation of new contract language to an impartial third party, whose decision, based upon the merits of the case, is final and binding. Interest arbitration, however, should not be confused with the topic of this book, namely, *rights arbitration*—the procedure wherein the parties submit a dispute involving the interpretation and application of existing contract language to the neutral party for final and binding resolution. Although interest arbitration is an interesting topic of study itself, and although much of what is said concerning rights arbitration may be applied to interest arbitration—for example, peaceful alternatives to strikes, arbitrator selections, hearing procedures, rules of evidence, and some decision-making principles—the focus of what follows is rights arbitration, or the arbitration of grievances.

HOW CASES GET TO ARBITRATION

Grievances can reach arbitration in three ways: The first, and most common, is for the collective bargaining agreement's grievance procedure to require final and binding arbitration as its final step. The second is by means of a *submission agreement*, a case-by-case agreement to arbitrate a particular dispute. As disputes arise during the day-to-day operation of the organization, the union and employer may decide that they are best handled through arbitration. If so, they will execute a submission agreement specifying the matter to be arbitrated. These written agreements also commonly specify the arbitrator or the agency through which an arbitrator is to be obtained. The third path to arbitration is through statutory requirement. For example, the Indiana State Personnel Act and Chapter 279 of the Code of Iowa provide for the final and binding resolution of specific types of disputes by professional arbitrators.

If the contract specifies arbitration as the final step of the grievance procedure, there must generally be a *demand for arbitration*, the request for arbitration by either party necessary to set the arbitration process in motion. Most often, the union is the demanding party. In such cases, after the final internal step of the grievance procedure has been exhausted, the contract will specify a time frame in which the union must inform management of its intent to proceed to arbitration. At that point, one or both parties are required to contact a previously selected arbitrator or an administrative agency to obtain a list of names of possible arbitrators. If the latter, the contract will require each side to alternately strike one name from the list containing an odd number of arbitrator names. The last name remaining on the list becomes the arbitrator of record.

Once the arbitrator is selected, the parties must schedule a time and place for the arbitration hearing. A dispute sometimes arises over the time and place of the hearing; if so, it becomes the first issue the arbitrator must resolve. Before proceeding to a detailed examination of this third-party dispute resolution technique, however, a few points made earlier concerning grievance procedures warrant repetition and elaboration.

THE INTERNAL DISPUTE RESOLUTION MECHANISM: THE GRIEVANCE PROCEDURE

The negotiated grievance procedure is the private mechanism through which labor and management attempt to resolve disputes concerning the application and interpretation of the labor agreement and, sometimes, matters of external law. The foregoing definition may do the procedure a disservice by making it appear much more straightforward and simple than it actually is. For example, the phrase "application and interpretation of the labor agreement" may lead one to conclude that the procedure concerns itself solely with disputes over the written language of the collective bargaining agreement. Quite the contrary, the written language ("four corners") of the contract constitutes but a portion, albeit the major portion, of the agreement between the parties. In addition, there is a body of past practice, which inevitably evolves in all labor-management relationships. Past practice refers to the customary methods the parties have mutually adopted and repeatedly used over time to operate the organization and resolve day-to-day problems. Unless excluded from consideration by clear and specific contract language, past practice is as binding upon the parties as the written language contained within the four corners of the labor agreement. It is truly the common law of the shop—*shop-common law*. Also generally falling within the proper scope of the grievance procedure are discipline and discharge, even though there may not be written contract language requiring discipline and discharge to be handled in any specific manner. All that is required is a contract provision that specifies just cause for discipline or discharge. Even where the contract makes no specific mention of just cause, the parties may adopt the just cause standard through past practice, thereby bringing discipline and discharge within the scope of the grievance procedure.

As previously noted, grievance procedures normally consist of a series of steps during which progressively higher ranking union and management officials meet and review the claims, counterclaims, facts, and circumstances surrounding disputes in an attempt to resolve them. Most grievance procedures contain three or four formal steps. In practice, most also contain an informal step prior to the initiation of formal grievance proceedings. Here, an employee who has a dispute with his or her supervisor is provided with the opportunity to meet with the supervisor in an informal setting to work out any problems they may have. If unsuccessful, the employee may bring the grievance to the attention of the first-line union official. This is normally the union steward or committeeperson. After listening to the employee's problem and the remedy sought, the union official will conduct an investigation to determine whether the contract has been violated and, if so, the facts and circumstances surrounding the violation. If it is determined that the grievance has merit, a meeting is arranged with the employee's immediate supervisor to discuss and attempt to resolve the problem. This meeting between the union steward or committeeperson and the employee's immediate supervisor constitutes the first formal step of the grievance procedure. Should this meeting fail to produce a mutually acceptable resolution of the complaints—that is, should the complaint be denied when the union believes it to be meritorious—the union may appeal it (move it) to the second formal step of the procedure. The process will then be repeated, this time with higher ranking officials representing both the union and management. Should all of the steps that constitute the private grievance procedure be exhausted without resolving the dispute, one of two things may happen: If the contract does not contain an arbitration/no-strike clause, the union may resort to economic warfare—the strike—to resolve the dispute. If the contract does contain an arbitration clause, and should either party so demand, the parties must proceed to arbitration to resolve their dispute.

ARBITRABILITY

At this stage, the specific language of the grievance-arbitration provision becomes important for determining whether the dispute can be properly resolved through arbitration. If it can, it is said to be arbitrable;

if it cannot, it is said to be nonarbitrable. Should either party challenge the arbitrability of an issue, the arbitrator must resolve this threshold dispute before proceeding to hear and to rule on the merits of the primary dispute.

Arbitrability challenges can either be *substantive* or *procedural* in nature. The former questions whether the subject of the grievance falls within the proper scope of the grievance-arbitration process and, hence, within the arbitrator's jurisdiction. Does the grievance concern an issue that labor and management have contractually agreed to exclude from the internal dispute resolution process? An affirmative answer makes the dispute nonarbitrable. Procedural challenges, on the other hand, question whether one of the parties has failed to follow the contractually specified requirements for the filing and processing of grievances, thereby disqualifying an otherwise arbitrable dispute from arbitration. Each type of challenge is considered below.

Substantive Arbitrability

The collective bargaining agreement holds the key to substantive arbitrability.[3] Labor and management frequently exclude certain employees and issues from coverage of the private dispute settlement machinery or arbitration. Probationary employees, for example, are routinely denied access to the grievance-arbitration procedure. A *probationary employee* is a newly hired employee who has yet to complete some specified time period of employment. Most contracts set this probationary time period between thirty and ninety days. The newly hired employee has few, if any, contractual rights during this time. The employee quite literally serves at the pleasure of the employer. Probationary employees typify what is meant by "employment at will." They may be disciplined and discharged for whatever reason the employer chooses—provided, of course, that the reason is not one of those prohibited by statute (e.g., race, religion, age, sex, etc.). Simply put, the just cause standard does not apply to these employees. Any complaints stemming from adverse employer treatment are not grievances under the terms of the labor agreement and, consequently, nonarbitrable.

The contractual definition of grievance determines the scope of the grievance-arbitration procedure—that is, what issues are arbitrable and which are not. Grievance-arbitration procedures are classified as broad or narrow according to whether the definition of grievance contained in the labor agreement is broad or narrow. Typical of a broad grievance-arbitration procedure is such language as:

> For purposes of this contract, a grievance is defined as any dispute arising between the union or any member of the bargaining unit, and the Employer and/or its representatives or agents.

This language makes almost all controversies between a member of the union and a member of management a grievance and, therefore, subject to resolution through grievance-arbitration. At the extreme, disputes having little or nothing to do with the labor-management relationship become the grist for the grievance-arbitration mill. Imagine, for example, the many interesting and amusing possibilities for grievances that might grow out of a romantic relationship between two employees, one a member of the bargaining unit and the other a representative of management. Labor and management, therefore, are well advised to carefully structure the definition of grievance to meet their mutual needs, otherwise, the grievance-arbitration machinery may become so bogged down with irrelevant disputes that it cannot achieve its intended purpose—the channeling of conflict to productive ends. Worse yet, at least from the perspective of management, rights and responsibilities central to the basic management function and efficient operation of the agency, duties which Justice Steward contended "lie at the core of entrepreneurial control,"[4]—may be transferred to the employees or the union through arbitration.

A narrow grievance definition limits the scope of the grievance-arbitration process. Representative of a narrow definition and, hence, a narrow grievance-arbitration procedure, is such language as:

> A grievance under this Article and for purposes of this agreement is defined to be:
>
> • A dispute between the Union and the Employer concerning the interpretation and/or application of this Agreement as it pertains to the terms and conditions of employment contained herein.
> • All disputes whose subject matter is not specifically governed by the terms of this agreement or is not a term or condition of employment is not the proper subject of a grievance.

Here, only those topics addressed by the labor agreement—the negotiated terms and conditions of employment—constitute the proper subject for grievances. Accordingly, only disputes involving these topics are eligible for resolution through the grievance machinery. This narrow language prevents the grievance procedure from becoming overburdened and limits union and employee encroachment of rights and responsibilities that should properly remain managerial prerogatives. Whether other issues lying outside "the core of entrepreneurial control" should or should not be the subject of grievances and, therefore, liable to dispute resolution through the grievance-arbitration procedure, will depend upon the specific needs of each bargaining relationship.

The arbitration clause itself may further limit the types of grievances that may be resolved through third-party decision making. As is the case with grievance definitions, arbitration clauses may be classified as broad or narrow. The arbitrator's authority has few limits when defined by clauses like the following:

> The arbitrator's grant of authority shall be to resolve any dispute placed before him or her in accordance with this Article. If the parties cannot mutually agree on the specific language of the issue before the arbitrator, the arbitrator shall frame the language of the issue after due consideration of both parties' cases and proposed issues.

While the foregoing example is unusually broad in its grant of decision-making authority to the neutral party, broad arbitration clauses empower the arbitrator to resolve the dispute in whatever manner he or she deems appropriate. Most arbitrators dislike the carte blanche authority provided by such clauses, because they provide far more leeway and latitude than does the contract. As a result, the contract becomes virtually useless as a guide to arbitral decision making, contrary to the intent of most parties at the time they negotiate a contract.

Narrow arbitration clauses typically use language such as:

> The arbitrator's authority shall be limited to the specific issue placed before him. The arbitrator shall have only the authority to interpret and apply the parties' Contract. The arbitrator shall not add to, subtract from, or modify, in any manner, the express terms of this Contract.

Here, the arbitrator must operate within narrowly prescribed limits. Only the issue or issues framed and submitted jointly by both parties may be considered, and then only to the extent that they require the interpretation or application of given contract provisions under specific sets of facts and circumstances. The arbitrator is forbidden from modifying or changing the express provisions of the contract in any way. Violation of the foregoing limitations may subject the arbitrator's award to court reversal on grounds that the arbitrator has exceeded his or her authority.[5]

Still other issues may be excluded from grievance arbitration by means of specific contract provisions, even if these issues properly meet the definition of grievance contained in the labor agreement. Labor and management may judge an issue so important and sensitive that they will refuse to substitute the judgment of an outsider for the judgment of those most familiar with and closest to the problem—their own. In such cases the parties are willing to bear the high cost of litigation and economic warfare rather than submit the matter to arbitration and thus lose control over it. For example, in the private sector, many local United Auto Worker (UAW) contracts specifically exempt disputes over work rules from grievance arbitration.

In summary, substantive arbitrability is determined by the parties through the language they make a part of the labor agreement.

Procedural Arbitrability

An otherwise arbitrable dispute may be rendered nonarbitrable by the failure to follow contractually prescribed procedures for filing or processing grievances. The contract establishes a time limit for the filing of grievances, most often five to thirty days from the date of the alleged contract violation, or from the date when the employee could have reasonably been expected to have become aware of the alleged violation, or from the date of the last occurrence where the alleged violation is ongoing in nature. Arbitrators have not hesitated to find disputes nonarbitrable where these time limits have not been met.

Once a grievance has been filed in timely fashion, all time limits specified by the contract for responses and appeals—that is, time limits for processing the grievance from one step to the next—must be met for it to remain timely and, therefore, arbitrable. Each step of the procedure establishes a time period during which the employer must respond to any grievance processed to that step as well as a time period during which the union must appeal any unsatisfactory response that it receives to the next step. Should the union fail to meet its deadline for appeal, most contracts provide for the automatic settlement of the grievance in accordance with management's last response. On the other hand, should management fail to meet its response deadline, most contracts provide for automatic movement of the grievance to the next step of the procedure. In the union's case, the grievance is considered settled and procedurally nonarbitrable,[6] whereas, in management's case, it remains procedurally arbitrable— active and eligible for settlement through arbitration. In practice, therefore, failure to meet procedural deadlines more often than not carries a more severe penalty for the union than for management.

Most contracts permit the extension of time limits through mutual agreement. To avoid costly disputes over whether filing and processing deadlines have been extended, and therefore whether grievances are procedurally arbitrable, all mutually agreed upon time limit extensions should be committed to writing. Without this paper trail, arbitrators will consider the time limits to have been unilaterally extended and violated and will rule the matter nonarbitrable. Such a violation is termed a violation of *laches*—that is, of timeliness.

Proper Specification of Charges

While improper specification of infractions of disciplinary work rules does not, technically speaking, render a dispute nonarbitrable, it does produce the same result, namely, a defective and "nonwinnable" dispute. Take the case of the postal letter carrier who was fired for "failure to follow the authorized line of travel as indicated on Postal Form 1066A." During his tour of duty, he stopped at a bar for lunch, drank five beers, became intoxicated, returned to his vehicle, and immediately proceeded to jump a curb and a five-foot ditch, landing squarely on top of a brand-new Chevrolet Corvette. While the grievant was guilty of many rules infractions for which discharge was proper, he was not guilty of what he was charged with. The charge was flawed in two respects: First, there was no Postal Form 1066A relevant to the matter and, second, there was no current line of travel authorized for the grievant's route, the last one having been filed in 1954. Since that time, new roads had been constructed and added to the route, and old ones had been bulldozed and deleted from the route. Hence, there was no current authorized line of travel on file. Such an improper specification of charges barred management from proceeding with evidence of intoxication, vehicular recklessness, property damage, trespassing, etc.—all of which carry the penalty of discharge, and all of which the grievant was guilty of committing. Such inaccuracy and misspecification benefits neither side. In the above example, the grievant went through two more defective discharge proceedings before finally killing himself in a traffic accident—on his own time.

ARBITRATORS AND PROCEDURAL ARBITRABILITY

As so often happens in arbitration matters, arbitrators take a variety of approaches to the issue of procedural arbitrability. Differences are essentially due to the importance accorded the arbitrator's source of authority and the effectiveness of arbitration as a dispute resolution technique.

Arbitrators who give the latter greater weight subscribe to the theory that form ought not control substance. They normally will not invoke the doctrine of laches unless the failure to be timely was intentional or adversely affected the contractual rights of one party or the other.

Arbitrators who give greater weight to the arbitrator's source of authority eschew inquiries concerning the reasons for the effects of the untimely filing or processing of grievances. While they believe that doubts as to the meaning of contractual time limits or whether they have been met should be resolved against forfeiture of the right to process the grievance, these strict contract constructionists hold that a clear failure to observe grievance filing and processing time limits will terminate the grievance. While the law may abhor forfeitures, they argue, the arbitrator is a creature of the contract, draws his or her authority therefrom, and must be bound by its clear language in rendering a decision. To do differently, they continue, would undermine the integrity not only of the arbitration process but the overall collective bargaining process as well; the contract would become meaningless, as would the process that created it.

Still a third group of arbitrators takes middle ground in the procedural arbitrability controversy. They will follow the loose contract constructionists when there is a broad grievance-arbitration procedure, and they will follow the strict contract constructionists where there is a narrow grievance-arbitration procedure. In a nutshell, the loose constructionists believe that too much legalism may destroy the characteristics that make grievance arbitration the effective dispute settlement mechanism that it currently is, whereas the strict constructionists believe that too much legal license may destroy the foundation of arbitration—the labor agreement—and the process which gave it birth—collective bargaining. There is something to be said for each point of view.

CONCLUSION

Grievances constitute the subject of rights arbitration. Grievances can get to arbitration through the requirements of the grievance procedure or by submission agreement. This, however, does not mean that they are arbitrable. For a grievance to be the proper subject of arbitration, it must meet both the procedural and the substantive requirements specified in the labor agreement for the arbitration of the dispute. Failure to meet either type of requirement renders the dispute nonarbitrable.

NOTES

1. For a more detailed discussion of mediation, see: Carl M. Stevens, "Mediation and the Role of the Neutral," in *Frontiers of Collective Bargaining*, ed. John Dunlop and Neil W. Chamberlain (New York: Harper & Row, 1967); George T. Sulzner, "The Impact of Impasse Procedures in the Public Sector: An Overview," *Journal of Collective Negotiations in the Public Sector* (1975), 4(1): 3–21; Kenneth M. Jennings, Jay A. Smith, Jr., and Earle C. Traynham, Jr., *Labor Relations in a Public Service Industry: Unions, Management, and the Public Interest in Mass Transit* (New York: Praeger, 1978); Stephen Briggs and Daniel J. Kays, "What Makes Labor Mediators Effective?" *Labor Law Journal* (August 1989), 40: 517–20; Sam Kagel and Kathy Kelly, *The Anatomy of Mediation: What Makes It Work* (Washington, D.C.: Bureau of National Affairs, 1989).

2. Charles O. Gregory and Harold A. Katz, *Labor and the Law* (New York: W. W. Norton, 1979), p. 233.

3. Unless the contract contains clear language to the contrary, the contract need only have either an arbitration clause or a no-strike clause for the courts to presume the existence of the other. Simply put, the NLRB and the courts have adopted a quid pro quo view of arbitration and no-strike clauses: the presence of one presumes the existence of the other. For the NLRB's rationale as it applies to the private sector, see: *Shell Oil*, 77 NLRB 206 (1948). State PERBs frequently follow the lead of the private sector in such matters.

4. *Fibreboard Paper Products v. NLRB*, 379 U.S. 203 (1964).

5. *Torrington Metal Products v. Metal Workers Local 645*, 363 F. 2d 677 (1966).

6. Appendix 1 contains an example of a case where the arbitrator determined a grievance to be procedurally nonarbitrable because the union failed to process it in a timely fashion.

Arbitration: Meaning, Types, Legal Foundation, Demographic Characteristics of Arbitrators, and Related Issues

This chapter examines the nature, varieties, and legal foundations of arbitration. It also examines the different agencies to which labor and management turn for the names of qualified arbitrators. The final section of this chapter examines the demographic characteristics of arbitrators— who arbitrators are and how they achieve party acceptability for dispute resolution.

NATURE AND VARIETIES OF ARBITRATION

Arbitration is that method of labor-management dispute resolution wherein the parties submit a dispute to an impartial third party for final and binding resolution. As noted in the preceding chapter, where the dispute concerns the creation of new contract language, this dispute resolution procedure is labeled interest arbitration, and where the dispute concerns the meaning and application of existing contract language, it is labeled rights arbitration. Interest arbitration is common in the public sector where unions generally do not have the right to strike, but rare in the private sector where unions do have the right to strike. Rights arbitration, on the other hand, is common to both public and private sectors. Most often it concerns disciplinary or contract interpretation matters.

Arbitration can also be classified as voluntary or compulsory. Arbitration is voluntary when labor and management have agreed, either by a collective bargaining contract or a separate submission agreement, to be bound by the decision of an impartial third party. Once they have struck such an agreement, however, there is no turning back; they are compelled to proceed to arbitration and to abide by the neutral's decision. Arbitration is compulsory where labor and management are mandated by statute to submit their disputes to a third party for final and binding resolution. While very rare in the private sector, it does exist in the railroad industry and has been used in certain defense-related industries during times of national emergency.

The widespread voluntary acceptance of arbitration as the preferred method of dispute resolution can be traced to its informality and relatively low cost. It is a quasi-judicial forum. Arbitration is much less formal than its first cousin because it does not rely on strict rules of evidence and rigid procedure, characteristics that not only make its relative more intimidating but more time consuming, expensive, and, hence, inaccessible. In short, arbitration is more accessible and less intimidating than its judicial counterpart.

THE LEGAL ENVIRONMENT OF ARBITRATION

Volumes have been written concerning the legal environment of arbitration. While interesting and stimulating from the perspective of the legal scholar, court official, or practicing attorney, union and management advocates need only be concerned with a few of the concepts and principles that comprise this extensive body of law. This is not to say that there will never be an occasion when a more extensive knowledge of the body of arbitration law would be helpful. There most assuredly will be such occasions, but they will be few and far between. Limitations of time and space dictate preparation for the rule rather than the exception. Accordingly, the following discussion is limited to those elements of arbitration law that will be useful to labor relations practitioners in the daily administration of the grievance-arbitration procedure. These elements of arbitration law are the enforceability of arbitration agreements and arbitration awards, the deferral of Unfair Labor Practice (ULP) disputes to private arbitration for resolution, and the duty to fairly represent bargaining unit members throughout the grievance-arbitration process.

The Enforceability of Arbitration: Agreements and Awards

The place of honor arbitration now occupies in labor-management relations as the preferred method of dispute resolution was not always guaranteed. Until 1957, whether collective bargaining contracts in general and arbitration agreements in particular were legally enforceable depended upon the state court having jurisdiction over the matter. Most state courts refused to enforce such agreements because they did not believe unions were legal personalities for contractual purposes. They did not believe the union had the authority to commit employees to any type of contract provision. In addition, the courts did not see the quid pro quo necessary for a valid contract. For them, the labor agreement represented a one-way transfer of benefits from the employer to the employees; they received nothing of comparable value from the union, only from individual employees. As Gregory and Katz have so succinctly observed:

> The courts found neither the technical consideration from the union to make the instrument a contract enforceable at law nor the mutuality of obligation necessary to make it specifically enforceable by the decree of a court of equity. Furthermore, the courts were quick to find restrictive or monopolistic provisions in these agreements and these, according to the general law of contracts prevailing among merchants, rendered them unenforceable as against public policy.[1]

It was in the midst of this legal fog that Congress enacted the Taft-Hartley Act of 1947. Section 301 of this statute in pertinent part states:

> (a) Suits for violation of contracts between an employer and a labor organization representing employees in an industry affecting interstate commerce, as defined in this Act . . . may be brought in any district court of the United States having jurisdiction of the parties, without regard to the amount of the controversy or without regard to the citizenship of the parties.

At first glance, this provision appears to make collective bargaining agreements in general and arbitration provisions in particular enforceable through the federal court system. Final determination, however, had to await Supreme Court action. Conceivably, as had occurred on previous occasions with several other statutes, the court could have interpreted the provision in a fashion contrary to the apparent meaning intended by Congress. The court settled the matter with its decision in *Textile Workers Union of America v. Lincoln Mills of Alabama* in June, 1957.[2] In this case, the parties had executed a collective bargaining contract containing an arbitration provision. The employer refused to proceed to arbitration, and the union brought suit under Section 301 of Taft-Hartley to compel arbitration. The Supreme Court voted to enforce the agreement to arbitrate, and, in doing so, established the Taft-Hartley Act as statutory authority for court enforcement of labor agreements.

Arbitration's role in labor relations was solidified and its relationship to the courts defined by three Supreme Court decisions rendered on June 20, 1960. These landmark decisions are commonly referred to as the Steelworkers Trilogy. In the first two cases, the *United Steelworkers v. Warrior and Gulf Navigation Company* and *United Steelworkers of America v. American Manufacturing Company*,[3] the Supreme Court took the position that, unless excluded from grievance arbitration by clear and specific contract language, all issues are arbitrable, not just those that a court may deem meritorious. Stated differently, arbitrability is a matter for the arbitrator to decide. In the third case, *United Steelworkers of America v. Enterprise Wheel & Car Corp.*,[4] the court held that the courts cannot overrule an arbitrator's decision simply because they disagree with his or her construction and interpretation of the labor agreement. The court reasoned that the arbitrator's opinion was bargained for, not that of the courts. The courts, therefore, exceed their authority whenever they substitute their judgment for that of the arbitrator. In short, the Supreme Court's decisions in the trilogy cases established arbitration as a legitimate method of dispute resolution not inferior to judicial processes.

Deferral to Arbitration

The NLRB and the Supreme Court have further enhanced the stature and scope of labor arbitration through deferral of jurisdictional authority. Many unfair labor practices are also issues that may be brought to grievance under most labor contracts. Such disputes simultaneously fall within the jurisdiction of the NLRB and the jurisdiction of the arbitrator; there is overlapping jurisdiction. Where this occurs, the NLRB frequently defers resolution of the unfair labor practice to the grievance-arbitration forum. The most notable exceptions are precedent-setting disputes, where the NLRB will retain its jurisdiction and resolve the dispute.

Purportedly initiated to encourage the parties to settle their differences by the method they voluntarily agreed to at the time of contract negotiation, the Collyer Doctrine,[5] as this policy of deferral has commonly become known, is highly controversial. Organized labor has vehemently opposed the policy on grounds that it encourages employers to violate federal labor law and that it internalizes the costs of enforcing federal law. The probabilities of a guilty verdict and of a substantial remedy are less under arbitration than under NLRB proceedings. Simply put, the probabilities of getting caught and the penalty when caught are less. Under arbitration, therefore, there is less deterrent to employer violations of federal law than under NLRB proceedings. In addition, according to organized labor, the enforcement costs are shifted from the taxpaying public to rank-and-file union members, because the costs of arbitration are, for the most part, shared by the parties to the labor agreement. In short, organized labor believes it has paid a disproportionately large share of the costs associated with what amounts to a successful attempt by the NLRB to reduce its caseload.

Despite the controversy surrounding deferral, the Supreme Court extended the same procedure to EEOC complaints. In its celebrated *W. R. Grace* decision, the Supreme Court established a policy whereby disputes that simultaneously involve matters of discrimination and contract interpretation may be resolved through arbitration, provided the contract prohibits discrimination.[6]

In summary, administrative law agencies and the courts have expanded the role of labor arbitration to include the enforcement of federal statutory law—that is, the NLRA, as amended, and the Equal Employment Opportunity Act—as well as the enforcement of private contract law.

The Limits of Arbitral Authority: Fair Representation

At first glance, it may appear that arbitration has become a law unto itself, that the process is not answerable to higher authority, and that the decisions of arbitrators are not subject to court review and possible modification or revocation. This is simply not the case; the arbitrator's decision and, hence, the entire process are subject to court review where: the arbitrator has failed to conduct a fair and proper hearing,[7] the arbitrator has clearly exceeded his or her authority as specified in the labor agreement,[8] the grievance involves violations of constitutional or statutory rights as well as contractual rights,[9] and the union has not discharged its obligation to fairly represent an employee. The latter is particularly germane to the present discussion.

The NLRA and other federal, state, and local statutes that provide for exclusive employee representation by labor unions for purposes of contract negotiation and contract or statute administration also require fair representation by those same unions. The right or privilege of exclusive representation carries the responsibility or obligation of fair representation—a quid pro quo relationship.

The duty to fairly represent involves both substantive and procedural requirements. It requires the union, when representing an employee during contract administration, to conduct a full and competent investigation of all matters pertaining to the grievance and to process or act upon the grievance in good faith without caprice or malice and without an intent to discriminate with regard to the grievant's race, sex, age, or union membership status.[10] Failure to meet any of these obligations may subject the union to a charge of failure to fairly represent and, ultimately, liability for back pay. Take, for example, the case of *Hines v. Anchor Motor Freight.*[11] Several employees were discharged for allegedly defrauding funds from their employer. Although the union processed their grievances through the grievance procedure to arbitration, it did not conduct an adequate investigation and competent defense in the case, leading the arbitrator to deny the grievances and uphold the discharges. After the arbitrator had issued his award, additional evidence was uncovered indicating that the employees were innocent. They then sued the company and union for reinstatement, back pay, and legal fees. The lower federal courts refused to vacate the arbitration award and reinstate the employees, citing the Supreme Court's decision in *United Steelworkers of America v. Enterprise Wheel & Car Corporation.*[12] The Supreme Court, however, reversed the lower courts, vacated the arbitration award, reinstated the employees, and apportioned damages (back pay and legal fees) equally between the employer and the union—the equal sharing of liability justified on the grounds that it was the employer who wrongly discharged the employees but the union who failed to secure prompt reinstatement through fair representation.

Good faith and honest and nondiscriminatory grievance administration, however, are not sufficient to protect the union from a charge of failure to fairly represent and the substantial costs possibly stemming therefrom. The union must also follow proper procedure, as established by the Supreme Court in *Bowen v. U.S. Postal Service* (1983),[13] in grievance administration. The case involved a wrongfully discharged employee who brought suit in federal district court against his employer, the U.S. Postal Service, for discharge without cause, and his union, the American Postal Workers Union, for arbitrary and capricious handling of the grievance, and for breaching its duty to fairly represent employees. The union had found the grievance to be without merit and decided accordingly not to process it to arbitration. Reversing an appellate court ruling for the union, the Supreme Court concurred with the federal district court that the union had not fairly represented the employee in the dispute. Interestingly, the court found specifically that the union: had honestly addressed the grievance, had not behaved in a malicious or capricious manner, had not discriminated on the basis of any illegal criterion, and had conducted a fair and full investigation of the matter. The union fell short, according to the court, in its failure to provide an explanation to the aggrieved employee for not proceeding to arbitration. The court reasoned that, had the union done so, the aggrieved employee could have countered the errors the union had, in good faith, made in determining the grievance to be without merit. The court then proceeded to uphold the federal district court's apportionment of damages (back pay) between the employer and the union. The employer was deemed liable for back pay from the time of unlawful discharge until the time when an arbitrator would have reinstated the employee had the union properly represented him, with the union liable for any back pay from that point onward.

Another procedural requirement for an employee to bring a successful suit against his or her union for failure to fairly represent concerns time limits. In *Del Costello v. IBT 113*, the Supreme Court adopted a six-month time limit for the initiation of such suits.[14] By doing so, the court provided unions some measure of protection from large back pay and damage awards; the employee cannot lay back and wait several years before filing in the hope of achieving what amounts to a paid vacation. In short, to be successful, suits for breach of fair representation must be filed in a timely fashion—within six months from time of the breach's occurrence.

A Good Rule of Thumb

Although the foregoing discussion has been couched primarily in terms of private sector labor relations, the public sector—be it federal, state, or local government—has followed the lead set by the private sector. Legislation that either provides for collective bargaining or arbitration is modeled after its private sector counterpart. Court interpretation of such legislation does not distinguish between sectors; where the law is the same, court interpretation is the same. Regardless of sector, the legal environment has become increasingly complex over time. Labor advocates, however, need not be intimidated by this complexity. Most difficulties can be avoided by adherence to a simple rule of thumb in grievance administration: use common sense. Be honest and act in good faith, do all that you can do for the grievant, treat all employees the same under similar sets of circumstances, and keep all discussions problem rather than personality centered. If you are unsure how to proceed, don't hesitate to seek the advice of higher-ranking union officials, particularly the international staff representative. In addition, most national unions have legal departments to which the local union official can come for expert legal advice. The old saw, "An ounce of prevention is worth a pound of cure," is as appropriate to grievance administration as it is to any other endeavor.

ARBITRATOR SELECTION:
THE ROLE OF THE ADMINISTRATIVE AGENCY

An *administrative agency* is an organization established to provide labor and management with a list of qualified arbitrators available to resolve their disputes. The most commonly used agencies in the private sector are the American Arbitration Association (AAA) and the Federal Mediation and Conciliation Service (FMCS). The National Mediation Board (NMB) performs the same function for labor and management in the airline and railroad industries. The FMCS and the NMB were created by the NLRA in 1935 and the Railway Labor Act in 1926, respectively, and are therefore government agencies. The AAA, on the other hand, is a private, nonprofit organization.

At first glance, these agencies may appear to perform a rather straightforward and simple function. Quite the contrary, it is much more complex. These agencies do not submit the name of just any arbitrator for the parties' consideration; they submit only the names of qualified arbitrators. Prospective arbitrators must meet certain minimum requirements, typically referred to as *standards of panel acceptability*, before their names are included on the agency's list, or panel of qualified arbitrators. The first of these requirements is that the prospective arbitrator subscribe to the standards of conduct contained in the *Code of Professional Responsibility for Arbitrators of Labor-Management Disputes*, a copy of which is included as Appendix 2 to this book. The candidate must also occupy a neutral position. Most frequently regarded neutral positions are those of college professor and private practice attorney. The final threshold requirement is that the prospective arbitrator be formally trained or have significant practical experience in labor relations matters, including sufficient knowledge of jurisprudence, to be able to conduct a fair arbitration hearing.

All three agencies noted above have additional requirements. For example, the FMCS requires prospective panel members to submit five arbitration opinions along with their applications, which are reviewed by the FMCS to ensure that the panel applicant has the ability to provide the parties with a logical, understandable, and well-reasoned explanation for any decision that he or she may make. In addition, the AAA requires its panel applicants to submit the names of a dozen or more labor relations practitioners—union advocates, management representatives, and established neutrals—who can attest to the applicant's neutrality and expertise in the labor relations arena. While the NMB does require substantial experience, it has not set a minimum number of arbitration cases or references as requirements for panel membership.

The FMCS, the largest of the agencies in terms of requests for panels of arbitrators, receives anywhere from twenty thousand to thirty-five thousand requests each year. Of these cases, approximately one-fourth are settled through the issuance of an arbitration award; the remainder are either withdrawn or settled privately between the parties. Each of the three major agencies gathers information on various aspects of the arbitration process—number of panels requested, number of cases cancelled and settled, types of disputes, whether arbitrability was an issue, whether briefs were filed and transcripts taken, expenses involved, elapsed time from grievance to panel selection, hearings, issuance of awards, etc.—and makes this information available to all interested parties upon request.

The AAA and the FMCS provide still another valuable service: rules and regulations for proper arbitrator conduct and procedures for a fair and impartial arbitration hearing.[15] These rules and procedures safeguard the integrity of the institution of arbitration as the preferred method of dispute resolution in two ways: First, they guarantee that the process will be swift, fair, and relatively inexpensive, thereby making and keeping it a more attractive dispute settlement alternative than either litigation or economic warfare. Second, these rules and regulations reduce the procedural and behavioral uncertainty of arbitration, and, in doing so, encourage its adoption by risk-averse practitioners. That they simply know what to expect in arbitration increases the likelihood that they will perceive the process to be fair and useful.

The arbitration clause of the labor agreement, or, in the absence of such a contract, the applicable statute or ordinance, will normally specify the administrative agency to be used for selecting an arbitrator. Ad hoc arbitration, as its name implies, refers to an arbitration proceeding wherein the arbitrator is selected after a dispute has arisen, the grievance procedure has not resulted in a successful resolution, and there has been a formal demand for arbitration. In ad hoc arbitration, the parties contact the administrative agency and request a list of names of qualified arbitrators. The FMCS or AAA will then forward a panel containing an odd number— most often between three and nine—of names, together with a brief resume for each arbitrator on the panel. Once the panel and biographical information are received, each side, taking turns, strikes the name of one arbitrator from the list. The contract specifies the party to strike first or the manner in which this party is to be chosen—normally by lot or coin toss. The process continues until a single name remains—the name of the arbitrator for the current dispute.

Administrative agencies also play a prominent role in the selection of a *permanent arbitrator* or *umpire*. A permanent arbitrator is a neutral selected by the parties, normally at the time of contract negotiation or shortly thereafter, to hear all cases arising during some specified period of time, usually the duration of the labor agreement. The permanent arbitrator is frequently selected from a panel of arbitrators provided by an administrative agency in precisely the same way an ad hoc arbitrator is selected. A notable exception occurs where the parties select a previous ad hoc arbitrator to serve in a permanent capacity, because the arbitrator has demonstrated his or her ability to resolve disputes impartially against the backdrop of technical requirements of the industry and the individual needs, personalities, characteristics, and circumstances that constitute the bargaining relationship. While the use of permanent arbitrators has become somewhat more common in recent years, the majority of private sector labor contracts provide for ad hoc arbitration. The majority of federal sector collective bargaining contracts, on the other hand, require the use of permanent arbitrators. One possible explanation may be the different experiences that the sectors have had with these two types of arbitration. Quite simply, ad hoc arbitration may have worked better for private bargaining relationships than federal ones.

Many states have established administrative law agencies to oversee—that is, administer, interpret, and enforce—collective bargaining legislation governing specific categories of public employees. In this regard, they are similar to the NLRB. In fact, they are often referred to as "little" NLRBs. Where they differ from their private sector namesake is that they also maintain a list of arbitrators available to public sector agencies and unions upon request. The Iowa PERB, Illinois Education Employment Relations Board, and the New Jersey Public Employee Relations Commission are examples of such agencies. It is not uncommon for these agencies to serve private sector employers and unions. The Indiana Division of Labor, for example, who has the responsibility of maintaining a list of arbitrators and keeping up-to-date biographical information for public sector labor disputes under the State Personnel Act, routinely provides arbitration panels to private sector unions and management. The sole advantage of using these state agencies is that they do not charge any fees for the information they provide. The FMCS and AAA, on the other hand, both charge fees for their services. The AAA currently charges seventy-five dollars to provide arbitration panels, schedule hearings, exchange briefs, and notify parties of the arbitrator's decision.

DEMOGRAPHIC CHARACTERISTICS OF ARBITRATORS

The old saw, "You get what you pay for," is probably as applicable, if not more so, to the services provided by state administrative agencies as to the services and products provided by any other public or private agency or firm. Simply put, these agencies do not thoroughly screen their applicants or maintain high standards for admission. As a result, almost anyone can claim to be an arbitrator, no matter how unqualified, and successfully gain appointment to many of these state agencies. What then distinguishes the qualified from the unqualified? The real test of an arbitrator is whether the individual is acceptable to the parties. *Party acceptability*—whether an individual is chosen as an impartial neutral to resolve a dispute—depends upon the quality of past services. Only those who have served their customers, labor and management, well are selected again.

There is a problem with this litmus test. Presumably, an arbitrator who is knowledgeable and capable of conducting a fair hearing and writing a well-reasoned opinion establishes party acceptability by repeatedly demonstrating these characteristics in his or her work. Herein lies the proverbial rub. How does an unknown but otherwise qualified neutral gain experience when experience is a prerequisite for selection? As Figure 4.1

Figure 4.1
The Vicious Cycle of Party Acceptability

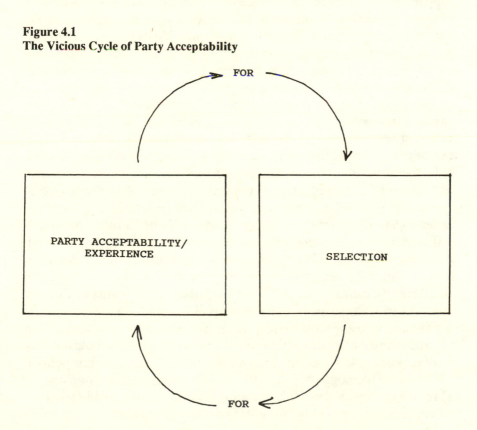

illustrates, there exists a vicious cycle, namely, party acceptability and experience depending upon selection and selection upon party acceptability and experience. This cycle, as are all such cycles, is difficult to break and the reason there are so few widely accepted arbitrators. As of January, 1988, the vast majority of all arbitration cases were heard by 680 arbitrators.

The National Academy of Arbitrators

These mainline arbitrators comprise the membership of the National Academy of Arbitrators (NAA), which is not an administrative agency like the AAA but rather a professional organization with very stringent admission requirements. To gain membership, an individual must be nominated by a current member, demonstrate party acceptability, and be elected by the membership committee. Demonstrated party acceptability entails no fewer than fifty cases involving at least ten different unions and ten different employers during the previous five years and letters of support from at least seven management and seven union advocates. In addition, the prospective member must have ten years of experience in the arbitration profession. In 1987, only thirty individuals met these demanding requirements and were admitted to the NAA. Each of these new members heard in excess of two hundred cases during the five-year time period preceding their election to the NAA.

Arbitration clauses frequently require that arbitrators selected to hear cases be members of the NAA. This is not surprising; NAA members are seasoned veterans who have established reputations for ethical conduct, fair hearings, sound reasoning, and quality awards. Sole reliance upon NAA members as arbitrators, however, does involve a cost. The calendars of NAA members are filled many months in advance. As a result, almost a year may pass before new cases can be scheduled, with disputes left to fester during the intervening period. The old cliché "Justice delayed is justice denied" is as appropriate here as elsewhere in the judicial system. Another cost of exclusive reliance upon NAA arbitrators is that such reliance limits the opportunities for young arbitrators to gain experience and thereby establish their worth. Finally, there are a number of highly qualified arbitrators who are not members of the NAA. Many of these are individuals whose primary occupation, like education, precludes them from devoting the amount of time necessary to meet the threshold requirement of hearing no fewer than fifty cases during a five-year time period.

Some other demographic characteristics of arbitrators are worth noting. This information has been taken from various reports and publications of the FMCS and the NAA. Almost two-thirds of arbitrators are either practicing or teaching attorneys. Those who are not attorneys are educators possessing a doctoral degree in either economics or industrial relations. Very few women have been able to establish party acceptability in this male-dominated profession. Of approximately seven hundred members of the NAA, for example, less than 8 percent are women. The figures are even lower for blacks and other minority groups. Nor has there been a significant improvement in recent years. In 1987, for example, of the thirty individuals extended NAA membership, only one was black and two were female. At first glance, the data showing gross underrepresentation of females and blacks in the profession may appear to be prima facie evidence of discrimination by the NAA. Closer examination, however, reveals that this is not the case; instead, it reflects the preferences of the labor relations practitioners who select arbitrators and thereby determine party acceptability—the litmus test for a qualified arbitrator and the threshold requirement for NAA membership. In this regard, the demographic make-up of the arbitration profession reflects the tastes and preferences—the prejudices—of those who use the services of the profession and not the arbitration profession itself.

A few other characteristics warrant comment. As might be expected in a profession where experience is critical, the average age of an NAA member is over sixty. Indeed, there are currently only two members who are less than forty years old. Finally, arbitrator charges averaged approximately $450 per eight-hour day in 1989, with the average case costing the parties almost $1,600.

Arbitrator Neutrality

Neutrality is defined by the *Code of Professional Responsibility* in Section 1 A.2, which states:

> An arbitrator must be as ready to rule for one party as for the other on each issue, either in a single case or in a group of cases. Compromise by an arbitrator for the sake of attempting to achieve personal acceptability is unprofessional.[16]

Neutrality does not require the arbitrator to be devoid of values, preferences, and personal standards—to be, so to speak, amoral. Such a perspective would be extremely naive. This, however, is a far cry from saying that arbitrators are prejudiced. Quite the contrary, while individual arbitrators will differ in the way they view particular issues, arguments, and evidence, all available evidence indicates that they are uncannily consistent in their respective views from case to case, not varying their decisions because of the sex, race, religion, age, etc. of advocates or grievants, or because of the side that labor or management takes on a specific issue, or because of expediency.[17] Those arbitrators who do engage in such behavior will be identified as such as they gain experience and will become unacceptable to one or both parties.[18]

Labor and management advocates attempt to capitalize upon this variety of views within the arbitration profession by carefully researching the past decisions of arbitrators and then selecting those arbitrators they believe share their views regarding specific issues in dispute. In this manner, they hope to increase their chances of a favorable decision. Scrutiny of arbitrators' past decisions for purposes of selecting the "right" arbitrator is fraught with danger: an arbitrator's published awards may not constitute a representative sample of all his or her awards or thinking. Counting the number of times an arbitrator ruled for the union and the number of times he or she ruled for management to determine neutrality is similarly dangerous. A fifty/fifty split in awards is not necessarily a valid measure of impartiality. Factors such as the issue in dispute, who bears the burden of proof, and whether the political and legal environments influence case processing must be considered in any evaluation of an arbitrator's neutrality.[19] Arbitrators make their decisions based upon the evidence before them and relevant contract language. Without complete knowledge of both, the parties may badly misjudge the thinking of any given arbitrator. A more productive and informative approach would be to read the books and articles published by the arbitrator to ascertain his or her views regarding specific issues and topics.

Another short-cut that does not involve the shortcomings of those discussed in the previous paragraph is to check for membership in the NAA. The vast majority of NAA members will be acceptable to both parties, but there are also many acceptable arbitrators who are not yet members. To use NAA membership as the criterion for selecting an arbitrator runs the risk of striking otherwise acceptable arbitrators.[20]

In summary, the more information the parties have concerning the views of specific arbitrators, the more likely they are to make an acceptable choice. Whether a particular case will be won or lost due to the selection of a particular arbitrator, however, is subject to much debate. Some cases may be won or lost because of the arbitrator selected, but, over a large number and range of cases, arbitrator selection will not significantly influence the win/loss rates.

CONCLUSION

Most union advocates and many management advocates are not attorneys. While there is no need for a law degree to be an effective arbitration advocate, a basic understanding of the legal environment is necessary.

The remaining chapters will explain the process of arbitration, including how arbitrators decide cases.

NOTES

1. Charles O. Gregory and Harold A. Katz, *Labor and the Law* (New York: W. W. Norton, 1979), p. 477.
2. *Textile Workers v. Lincoln Mills of Alabama*, 77 S.Ct., 913 (1957).
3. 363 U.S. 574 (1960); 363 U.S. 564 (1960).
4. 363 U.S. 593 (1960).
5. *Collyer Insulated Wire*, 192 NLRB 837 (1971); *United Technologies Corp.*, 268 NLRB 83 (1984).
6. *United Rubber Workers, Local 759 v. W. R. Grace, Inc.*, U.S. 757 (1983).
7. *Spielberg Manufacturing Company*, 112 NLRB 1080 (1955).
8. *Torrington v. Metal Product Workers Local 645*, 363 F., 2d 677 (1966).
9. *Alexander v. Gardner-Denver Co.*, 415 U.S. 36 (1974).
10. *Vaca v. Sipes*, 363 U.S. 171 (1967).
11. 424 U.S. 554 (1976).
12. 363 U.S. 593 (1960).
13. *Bowen v. U.S. Postal Service*, 459 U.S. 212 (1983).
14. 462 U.S. 151 (1983).
15. See Appendix 3.
16. See Appendix 2.
17. Joseph P. Cain and Michael J. Stahl, "Modeling the Policies of Several Labor Arbitrators," *Academy of Management Journal* (1983), 26: 140–47.
18. Orley Ashenfelter, "Arbitrator Behavior," *American Economic Review* (May 1987), 77: 342–46.
19. In a sample of published cases from the Bureau of National Affairs and the Commerce Clearing House, it was found that unions prevail about 56 percent of the time in discharge and disciplinary matters, simply because management bears the burden of proof. On the other hand, in contract interpretation matters where the union bears the burden of proof, management prevails about 57 percent of the time.
20. For a further discussion of this issue, see: J. Timothy Sprehe and Jeffery Small, "Members and Nonmembers of the National Academy of Arbitrators: Do They Differ?" *The Arbitration Journal* (September 1984), 39: 25–33.

5

Procedure and Evidence in Rights Disputes

This chapter presents the procedures typically used by arbitrators in conducting hearings. The arbitration hearing will be familiar to jurists, but it is far less formal than civil or criminal proceedings. The rules of procedure used in courts are relied upon heavily by arbitrators to give the process predictability and structure. The more technical and formal aspects of courtroom rules are typically not applied in arbitration for efficiency and to assure that nonattorneys understand what is happening.

This chapter will examine the order of proceedings, including activities preliminary to the actual hearing, and the rules governing hearings. It is true that arbitrators differ somewhat on the application of certain procedural rules; however, where these differences are common they will be identified in the appropriate places in the discussion. In the final portions of this chapter the implications of procedural issues for case preparation are identified and explored in some detail.

Hearing procedures are very important to the advocate in any arbitration matter. Unless procedure is mastered and fully understood an advocate cannot possibly prepare or present an adequate case. Procedural violations can limit what evidence can be used and may result in less than efficient preparation for a case. In advocacy proceedings, if the respective parties are not adequately and fairly represented, then justice cannot have been done.

PROCEDURE

Procedure is the term used to describe the order of proceedings and the rules that will govern the hearing process. Arbitration is a quasi-judicial dispute resolution technique and therefore has procedural characteristics typically associated with courtrooms, although it is generally less formal. A standard position representing the views of a majority of neutrals will be presented, with occasional comments concerning prominent alternative approaches to hearing organization and rules. There appears to be the greatest agreement among neutrals as to the order of proceedings, and this area will be examined before moving to other aspects of procedure.[1]

Order of Proceedings

The *order of proceedings* is the chronology of events set in motion when a case goes to arbitration. The typical order of proceedings is outlined in the following list:

1. Prehearing conference
2. Prehearing stipulations and motions
3. Opening arguments
4. Presentation of respective parties' cases
5. Closing arguments or posthearing briefs
6. Posthearing stipulations and motions

The order of proceedings presented above is almost universally accepted by practicing labor arbitrators, except where law or the contract requires a different order.

The prehearing conference and posthearing stipulations and motions are particularly likely to be waived. On the other hand, some of the steps may assume unusual prominence. A prehearing conference might take several hours if the case is complex. Moreover, some arbitrators deviate from the order of events outlined here. These deviations are rarely extensive, but may be important in particular cases. Therefore, the outline ought to suggest an array of possibilities rather than a strict agenda.[2] With this in mind, the steps can be explored in some detail.

Prehearing Conference

The prehearing conference is just what the name implies—a conference between the neutral and the parties prior to the formal hearing. This conference offers an opportunity for the arbitrator to gather some of the information necessary to conduct the hearing. Arbitrators need to know what issues are in dispute, whether the parties intend to call witnesses, and, if so, whether the witnesses should be sworn or sequestered, or whether the parties have any stipulated facts or evidence they wish to have on the record as joint exhibits. In addition, the arbitrator will generally take a few minutes to explain how he or she is going to conduct the hearing. (More than a few minutes may be needed if the parties are new to the process.)

The handling of witnesses is very important. In some cases, witnesses are *sequestered*. This means holding them outside of the hearing room and keeping them separate so that they cannot hear one another's testimony or communicate with witnesses who are yet to testify. The reasons for sequestering witnesses vary, but the most common reasons are that there is an element of credibility in the cases, or that a witness's presence may be felt to have an intimidating effect on other witnesses. This motion, when made by either party, is generally granted.

In a strict legal sense, sequestration requires that each witness be isolated from all other witnesses. In arbitration it is rare that strict sequestration is requested or ordered. Usually, witnesses are excluded from the hearing room. There are exceptions to the separation of witnesses. For example, each advocate may request an assistant. This is especially true of outside attorneys who will want the local union president or personnel manager present, because the assistants will be much more familiar with the opposing parties' witnesses and the facts and circumstances surrounding a grievance or involved in the bargaining relation. In almost all cases the grievant will be permitted to remain in the hearing room, especially if the case involves disciplinary action.

The swearing in of witnesses may also be requested. If a party fears that a witness may not tell the truth, or believes that the witness might be intimidated into giving more complete testimony by the administration of the oath, he or she will typically move that the witnesses be sworn in. If a court reporter is present to make a transcript of the hearing, he or she has the authority to administer the oath.

Getting stipulations agreed to and into the record is a very important part of the prehearing conference. A stipulation, as noted previously, is an agreement between the parties that something is fact, or at least that it is not in dispute. This can save valuable time during preparation and the hearing itself. The arbitrator does not need to take evidence into the record concerning those issues, and does not need to give consideration to those problems that would follow normally, had the issue been the subject of disagreement.

This prehearing conference may sound like a trivial preliminary to the arbitration process, but it can be very important in complex cases, even though rarely conducted in simple matters. Finally, most neutrals will ask the parties if they have any concerns they would like to express, or questions that should be explored before the hearing. For example, if a witness has to be called out of order, or refuses to honor a subpoena, these matters are at this point properly addressed to the neutral.

Prehearing Stipulations and Motions

Most of the standard prehearing stipulations and motions have been examined in the section above. Three others are of particular importance, however, and deserve attention: motions for continuances, questions concerning whether one or more of the issues under consideration are properly before the arbitrator, and challenges to the neutral.

A *motion for continuance* is made when one or both parties for some reason want the hearing delayed. A request of this kind is typically made prior to the prehearing conference and often before the scheduled hearing date. It is much less common for such motions to be made after the prehearing conference but before the hearing. In extreme cases, it may be made during the hearing itself. When a motion for continuance occurs during the hearing it is generally because of problems in acquiring documents or of surprises that may occur during a witness's testimony. One particularly interesting example of a request for continuance during a hearing happened to one of the authors. During a rather heated exchange between the advocates, the union advocate suffered a stroke. As luck would have it, the local union requested a continuance, but the management advocate objected, on the basis of the union's "cheap theatrics." Normally an arbitrator will, as he did in the above example, grant a motion for continuance if the moving party has good cause. Neutrals will usually grant a continuance for any cause beyond the parties' control likely to have an effect on the fairness or result of the procedure. If, for example, important witnesses or documents are unavailable, that is usually regarded as sufficient to justify a continuance. On the other hand, requests for delays because a manager's child is ill, or a spouse's birthday is imminent, will generally not be honored.

The second important issue concerns whether a case or particular issue is properly before the arbitrator. If arbitrability is an issue, one or both parties will often ask to proceed separately on this issue before moving to the case on merits. This provides for a clear understanding of the arbitrability issue unburdened with facts and arguments concerning the merits of the case. Neutrals may ask if the parties are willing to stipulate that the present case is properly before him or her, just to make certain that there are no hidden legal difficulties.

Finally, the neutral may be challenged if a conflict of interest or unethical conduct is suspected.[3] These challenges should be made at the earliest possible time, generally before the prehearing conference but certainly before the hearing, and should be brought directly to the neutral. If a satisfactory explanation cannot be provided and the neutral refuses to remove him- or herself from the case, the matter should be taken to the administrative agency. The need for this is extremely rare, as most professional neutrals will withdraw from a case when either party requests it.

With these matters resolved, the parties can move to the hearing itself. The hearing has three major phases, beginning with opening arguments.

Opening Arguments

After the arbitrator brings the hearing to order, the opening argument is heard. It is, as the name suggests, the beginning of a party's case presentation. The opening argument should clearly and succinctly state the party's position on the issues and why its position ought to be regarded as more consistent with the available facts and evidence than the other party's position. Many, probably most, arbitrators prefer to have a statement of the party's position on each issue presented to them at the beginning of the hearing. This serves roughly the same purpose as a program in a play or at a ball game: it lets the arbitrator know what's coming next and how everything is supposed to fit together.

The party obligated to proceed first is normally the party bearing the burden of proof. In disciplinary and discharge matters it is the employer; in contract interpretation cases it is generally the union. Frequently the party required to proceed second will wish to reserve its opening argument until presentation of their case in chief. Most arbitrators will permit such reservation of opening arguments.

There are circumstances, however, when the moving party is not obliged to proceed first. In Indiana, state employees have the right to have complaints heard by a neutral arbitrator under certain circumstances. Under the original Indiana Personnel Act, the employee was the moving party regardless of the issue. The legislature amended the act to remove this requirement because of the extreme complications and expense involved in this illogical approach, but a few negotiated contracts still have such requirements.

Advocates should remember that the purpose of an opening statement is to let the neutral know what the party wants, and what, in their judgment, the evidence will demonstrate that it is entitled to receive. Opening arguments should be brief and focus clearly upon these points.

Presentation of Respective Parties' Cases

Once the opening arguments are completed, each party, in the same order, will be given an opportunity to present its *case in chief*, which is the presentation of evidence and testimony to support a party's initial position. (The term "initial position" recognizes the possibility that a party's position or contentions may change over the course of a hearing.)

The courtroom rules of evidence and procedure do not normally apply to arbitration. Although jurists would probably recognize the procedures used in these hearings as an approximation of the courtroom rules, the process is somewhat less restrictive. Hearsay testimony, leading questions on direct examination, depositions, and many other techniques that would not be allowed in court are common in arbitration, but they are sometimes self-defeating, as will be addressed later. We will examine the rules of evidence in detail later in this chapter. For the present, the point is simply that these hearings are somewhat less formal than courtroom proceedings.

When witnesses are used, the party calling the witness has an opportunity to examine that witness fully before yielding. This is called direct examination. Then the responding party has the opportunity to examine the witness fully. This is called cross-examination. If, after cross-examination is completed, the advocate who called the witness has additional questions to put to the witness, that advocate will be given an opportunity to question the witness further. This is called redirect examination. This process continues until both advocates are satisfied that they have gleaned all of the relevant testimony from the witness. At that time, the witness is either excused, or excused subject to recall, meaning that the witness might be examined again later in the hearing by one or both parties or called in rebuttal. Once the party obliged to proceed first has completed its presentation, the other party will be given the same opportunity to argue its case.

Documentary evidence is frequently used in arbitration cases. In the courtroom, the normal procedure for introducing documentary evidence is to call a credible witness who did not prepare the document, but who is familiar with it or is an expert concerning the data or the issue. This witness is asked to identify the source of the evidence and explain its significance. Although arbitration hearings allow advocates to proceed much less formally, it is not typically in their interest to do so. Establishing the credibility and significance of documents is very important. The evidence very possibly will not have the meaning, and often cannot be given the weight, that a proper presentation might gain for it. It is always wise to present documents in a manner that protects and clarifies their proper value.

Although the courtroom rules of evidence and procedure are not typically followed in any very rigorous sense, the presentation of an arbitration case in chief has much in common with the presentation of a case in court. As explained above, each party may call witnesses and introduce documentary or physical evidence. Objections may be raised and dealt with at any time, and the opposing party may cross-examine witnesses. Once the party obligated to proceed first rests its case in chief, the opposing party is given an opportunity to present witnesses and evidence.

If a party is surprised by elements of the opposing party's case in chief, or if a matter of credibility arises, it is not uncommon for a rebuttal opportunity to be requested. Most arbitrators allow this, but the rebuttal should be limited to those issues that the opposing party presented during its case in chief. It should not be used to present new lines of argument or new evidence.

Closing Arguments or Posthearing Briefs

Closing arguments, the final stage of the hearing, are often called summations because the advocates provide a summary of the evidence and the parties' positions on each issue. The skillful and sophisticated advocate limits his or her remarks to a summary of the arguments presented and an outline of the supporting evidence. Too often, less experienced advocates attempt to enter new evidence into the record or otherwise misuse the closing argument, which is expected to be a summary of the case. Very few arbitrators permit it to be used to extend the case in chief, or to modify the arguments introduced in rebuttal.

It is usually permissible for the closing argument to be used to attack the opposing party's case. The learned advocate will discredit the opponent's position by unemotionally and categorically refuting each of the opponent's claims. The advocate will point out the faults in the opponent's arguments and the weaknesses in the supporting evidence. The sophistication required to accomplish this can only be acquired by studying the process carefully and at length. The capacity to apply that sophistication to good effect requires that the advocate be fully prepared and pay close attention to events during the hearing.

The parties present their closing arguments in turn, with the party requesting the affirmative action again proceeding first. Often parties make their closing arguments, listen to the opponent's arguments, and then request an opportunity for rebuttal. Such rebuttals are time consuming and generally result in the opponent requesting the same consideration. This is not a constructive approach in most cases, and should not be regarded as the norm. On the contrary, rebuttal should be reserved for those occasions when it is truly needed. Experienced participants know that these are exceedingly rare.

It is not uncommon for the parties in an arbitration case to ask that the neutral accept case citations as a portion of the closing argument. This is a generally accepted practice. Most neutrals will accept not only case citations but copies of entire arbitration awards or court decisions. These are entered to provide the neutral with the benefit of other neutrals' reasoning concerning similar issues. Such precedents are not binding, but they are often helpful.

Occasionally parties will waive oral closing arguments in favor of submitting posthearing briefs, which are simply closing arguments in written form. There are several reasons why this written form may be preferred. The most straightforward and least interesting reason is that some advocates write better than they speak. Beyond that, complex issues, which frequently involve difficult legal questions, may be easier to follow in written form than in oral argument. If briefs are to be substituted for oral arguments, the mechanics for the parties' exchange of briefs must be agreed upon and deadlines for the submission of briefs set before the hearing is adjourned.

Posthearing Stipulations and Motions

Posthearing stipulations and motions are relatively rare, but several interesting ones are at least occasionally encountered. If posthearing briefs are to be filed, one party or the other may find that it is unable to meet the deadline specified and will ask for an extension. Such requests should be made in writing, where possible, with a copy to the opposing party. Direct contacts with the neutral should be avoided until the award is issued. If time does not permit the request to be made in writing and a party must contact the neutral by telephone, a conference call should be employed so that the other party can participate. At the very minimum, the opposing party's advocate should be informed in advance that the call will be made and what it is about. In fact, after the hearing is adjourned most neutrals will not accept a telephone call unless it is a conference call.

There are numerous other instances of posthearing motions and stipulations. One of the more interesting of these is a request for the clarification of an arbitration award. This is a request for an explanation of a portion of the award believed to have an uncertain meaning, or a correction of a portion believed to be in error. The Uniform Arbitration Code allows for clarification on the motion of either party or a court order. In practice, however, these clarifications are uncommon, unless the parties request them jointly. The *Code of Professional Responsibility* shared by the NAA, the AAA, and the FMCS restricts clarifications to those made by joint request. Most arbitrators will adhere to this recommendation, even if they are not members of the NAA or are not serving on the panels of the FMCS or AAA.[4]

This very conservative approach is probably justified. Many arbitrators have heard cases in which one of the parties has attempted to use the clarification process as a method of appeal or relitigation of the issues already settled. Arbitrators generally take great care to assure the integrity of the process and will not give a losing party an opportunity of this kind.

Another interesting use of posthearing stipulations concerns the neutral's desire to have information unavailable at the time of the hearing. Neutrals rarely request additional information, but if the information is not immediately available, the parties may agree to obtain and submit it to the neutral after the close of the hearing. This procedure is not uncommon. If the parties find they cannot stipulate to this additional evidence, they may submit their own versions of the requested information. When this occurs, each party must provide its version of the evidence to the other party as well as to the neutral, informing the latter that there is a dispute concerning the accuracy of the respective parties' data.

Other Procedural Issues

There are a great many other procedural issues associated with the arbitration process. Many of these are very technical legal issues only occasionally important in arbitration cases. These include vacation of arbitrator's awards, appeals to the courts, and enforcement orders. These matters cannot be given adequate attention here and are therefore not examined.[5] Several other less technical procedural issues are more common to arbitration, and these ought to be examined briefly. They include ex parte communications and hearings, subpoenas, stays and continuances, and inspections or site visitations.[6]

Ex Parte Communications and Hearings

Ex parte means, literally, in absence of one party. Ex parte communications are communications between one party and the neutral when the other party is absent. Similarly, an ex parte hearing is a hearing from which one party is absent. This imbalance raises issues of critical importance to most neutrals. Their reputation for fairness and lack of bias is the foundation upon which a career as an arbitrator must be built. Obtaining a fair and impartial hearing should also be of critical importance to the parties. Plainly, then, ex parte communications are undesirable. Neutrals and the parties share an obligation to keep ex parte communications to a minimum and to refrain from discussing the merits of arguments or cases on those occasions when ex parte communications are unavoidable. Most neutrals will instruct the parties to refrain from mentioning anything about pending cases during these communications, and responsible advocates take equal care.

Ex parte hearings are usually a different matter. If proceeding ex parte becomes an issue, it is almost always because one of the parties refuses to participate. Generally, where ex parte proceedings are allowed, neutrals will refuse to convene the hearing unless the absent party is fully aware that the hearing will proceed without them.

An ex parte hearing does not assure the participating party of victory. Neutrals will still require them to make a convincing case, effectively supporting their contentions. If they are unable to do so, they are almost certain to receive an unfavorable ruling. A party that refuses to participate does itself no favors, but there is no such thing as winning by default in arbitration as in the courts or with some administrative law agencies.

Subpoenas

A *subpoena* is an order to appear issued by an official given such power and authority by statute. The appearance can be as a direct witness or as a keeper of records. In the latter case, one can be required to produce those records for introduction into the record of the case or for inspection by the arbitrator or other party. Most states have adopted the Uniform Arbitration Act, and arbitrators operating within those states have subpoena powers. It is interesting to note that some states, like Kansas, exempt public sector employers and unions from applying the Uniform Arbitration Act.

Continuances and Stays

Continuances and stays are motions to delay the hearing or the appearance of one of the parties. It is not uncommon for a party to face obstacles—weather conditions, illnesses, and a variety of other circumstances—that would make attendance at a scheduled hearing impossible or unfair. Neutrals have their own requirements and preferences, but, in general, if there is good cause clearly out of the moving party's control, and there is no statutory prohibition against the continuance or stay, it will be granted. Similarly, if an unanticipated argument or piece of evidence is introduced, the neutral may grant the surprised party a continuance. The likelihood of this is roughly proportional to the degree to which the surprise could not reasonably have been foreseen. In cases where the surprise evidence is withheld willfully during the grievance procedure, such evidence is generally inadmissible. In general, whenever a continuance seems required to assure a fair hearing, a majority of neutrals will grant the motion. Because the desire to assure fairness is stronger than the desire to prevent abuses, continuances and stays are relatively common.

Inspections and Site Visitations

Occasionally an issue focusing on a specific work location will be presented in an arbitration case. In road maintenance, manufacturing, and postal operations, for example, the immediate work environment may be very important to understanding a party's case. Safety issues are particularly likely to require firsthand inspection of the site. For example, in a recent case an employee was charged with failure to observe safety rules because he threw a heavy metal part at a wall. The wall was next to a scrap bin in a corner where employees did not go. The union argued that the location of the bin and its proximity to other employees was relevant and therefore should be seen, firsthand, by the arbitrator. This can be time consuming and even costly if the site is far from the hearing location. However, the concern for fairness outweighs other factors. When both parties agree on the need for an inspection, arbitrators will almost certainly grant the motion. Even if one party objects, arbitrators will usually grant the motion if there is a reasonable link to the case. The delay and potential expense involved in these inspections is not as important to most arbitrators as their duty to assure a fair and impartial hearing.

RULES OF EVIDENCE

As noted, courtroom rules of evidence are not usually required in arbitration cases. Still, arbitrators rely heavily upon these rules for guidance. Even if they are somewhat less stringent than the courtroom rules, there is considerable structure to the rules of evidence in arbitration; therefore, an awareness of these rules is an important component of effective preparation. The most important of these rules concern examining witnesses and introducing documents.

The Examination of Witnesses

Generally speaking, a witness is a person called upon to offer firsthand testimony concerning events or to identify documents and other physical evidence about which they have knowledge. There are several special categories of witnesses: *Expert witnesses* may not have any direct knowledge of any relevant event, but they are trained and recognized experts in relevant subjects. For example, a certified public accountant or financial expert may be called to shed light on budgetary matters, or an industrial engineer on productivity matters.

Hostile witnesses are known to be unfriendly to the calling party's position. These witnesses are often handled differently from normal witnesses; for example, they may have to be subpoenaed and the neutral may have to instruct them to answer questions. It is also common for the advocate calling such witnesses to be allowed greater freedom in examining them. They may be allowed to employ leading questions to an unusual degree, for example. The following discussion focuses on the examination of a normal witness.

The advocate will first ask a witness called to the stand to identify himor herself. The witness should be asked to state his or her name and address and identify the nature and longevity of his or her links with either party. Expert witnesses should be asked to identify their area of expertise, their experience and training, and any honors they may have earned in that area. Once the witness is identified, direct examination should proceed to substantive questioning.

On direct examination the witness should be asked questions that demonstrate clearly how and why he or she came to have knowledge of the events at issue, to lay a foundation for the substantive testimony to follow. For example, if an advocate is going to call the union steward to testify concerning some aspect of the processing of the grievance, the advocate should ask if he or she attended the grievance meetings. If the steward says yes, the advocate should ask why. The witness will respond that he or she was the grievant's representative. This provides a foundation for and some perspective of the steward's testimony concerning the course of the grievance meetings. In a courtroom, such foundations must be constructed before substantive questioning takes place. In arbitration this procedure is not usually required, but it is a good idea to employ it. The neutral can best assign appropriate weight to testimony when he or she knows how the witness acquired the knowledge.

On direct examination the advocate should keep leading questions to a minimum. A *leading question* is a statement of fact to which the witness is asked to agree or disagree. For example, the advocate might ask, "You are the best employee this company ever had, correct?" The proper way to ask this question is, "Have you ever been cited by the company for outstanding contributions?" Most arbitrators will permit leading questions on direct examination, but only to a point. If it becomes clear that the advocate is testifying, rather than the witness, the questioning will almost always be stopped. If the opposing party objects to the leading of a witness, the neutral will often sustain the objection, because the testimony may be critical to the case and the opposing advocate's cross-examination may depend on the proper direct examination of the witness. Leading questions on cross-examination are permissible, within broad limits, even in a court of law.

Some standard tactics are used with witnesses. *Impeachment of a witness*, accomplished by discrediting a witness's testimony, is typically done on cross-examination by an opposing advocate. If an advocate can get a witness to change his or her testimony, or to admit that parts of it were speculative, then that witness's testimony will become suspect. How much the testimony must change or how severe the inconsistency must be to have a significant effect upon credibility is not subject to specific rules. Impeachment depends upon the neutral's perceptions.

Corroboration of testimony is where another witness or additional evidence can be adduced in support of existing testimony. If a witness claims to have observed two men meeting in the parking lot of a building, this testimony can be directly corroborated by another eyewitness testifying that he or she observed the same meeting. Corroboration does not depend upon identical observations. It may be enough, for example, for a witness to testify that he saw one of the two men entering the parking lot shortly before the meeting allegedly occurred, and yet another witness to testify that she saw the other man leave the parking lot shortly after the meeting allegedly occurred. The testimony of these two witnesses places the two men in the parking lot at the time the first witness claimed they met.

Witnesses can also be used to identify and describe the sources of documents, to explain how documents were created, and how and where they were stored.

Hearsay testimony is where one person testifies that he or she heard another person say something. In courtrooms such testimony is typically excluded. In arbitration proceedings, hearsay is normally allowed into the record, but not on an equal footing with other testimony. It will be given consideration to the extent that it is either corroborated or credible, but it will not be weighted as heavily as eyewitness testimony.

Witness preparation is a critical part of any case preparation. An advocate should never ask a question to which he or she does not already know the answer. It is wise to prepare, in advance, a list of questions to be asked on direct examination, and then put those questions to the witness at a prehearing meeting. As the witness answers the questions, the advocate should take notes concerning the witness's answers. The advocate should then assume the role of the opposing advocate and cross-examine the witness. This serves two important purposes: to see how well the witness's testimony will withstand cross-examination, and to give the witness some idea of what to expect when he or she testifies. This will prevent shock on the witness stand and make the witness appear more credible.

One of the most common mistakes that advocates make is the parading of witnesses. A party may call dozens of witnesses to testify to the same thing or to offer only very small increments of additional information, much of which may be tangential to the case at hand. One should remember that the quality of evidence is more important than the quantity. The parading of witnesses is tedious and expensive. Moreover, it may result in unexpected and damaging conflicts, which will undermine the advocate's case. It is better to call two witnesses who can provide the precise testimony needed in a credible manner than to call a crowd of witnesses to offer redundant versions of the events under review.

Documentary Evidence

In many cases, particularly those having to do with technical contractual issues, witnesses may not be the primary source of information. Instead, documents are asked to carry a great deal of the evidentiary burden. Even in those cases employing a substantial number of witnesses, documents may carry a significant part of the load. As a result, rules concerning the use of documentary evidence have been developed to parallel those dealing with the examination of witnesses.

Documents are typically divided into two categories in arbitration cases: business records and the statements of persons. Business records are generally admissible in both the courtroom and in arbitration. Labor contracts (both current and prior), budgets, work rules, and production schedules are all generally regarded as business records and are admissible. It is not uncommon for both labor and management to produce their own and different versions of certain records. In a case argued before the author, management and the union introduced completely different versions of the expiring contract under which they had been working. This was a new bargaining relationship, and each party truly believed the contract it presented had been negotiated the year before. This case was extremely complicated, primarily because the parties had no idea what they were doing. It was finally necessary to rule that references to the old contract would be limited to those cases in which the same language was to be found in both versions. Fortunately, disagreements as fundamental as this are uncommon. Typically, business records will be stipulated to and entered into the record as joint exhibits by the parties.

The statements of persons can take many different forms. *Depositions*, *Affidavits*, and *Interrogatories* are different forms of written testimony. Affidavits and depositions, usually considered hearsay testimony, present a special problem. An affidavit is a statement provided by a witness or expert, and a deposition is a set of answers provided by a witness or expert in response to specific questions posed by one of the advocates. The opposing side has no opportunity to cross-examine the author of such documents. For this reason, arbitrators do not usually admit them, unless there is some unusual and compelling reason to do so, like the death of the author or something of that kind. The cross-examination problem is circumvented in the case of interrogatories, which amount to a simple time shifting of the usual process. Both advocates are permitted to put questions to the witness, assuring the balance that may be absent in the case of depositions and affidavits.

Written notes taken during negotiations sessions or other meetings are not generally admitted into the record of a hearing. Arbitrators typically allow witnesses to refer to their notes while on the witness stand, and they are subject to inspection by the opposing advocate. Testimony from notes, however, may not be weighted as heavily as a witness's recall.

On occasion other statements from persons are offered for admission into the record. One of the most common documents in this category is the newspaper article or editorial. Arbitrators differ on the admissibility of such documents. If they are offered as proof of facts, most neutrals will not accept them. If, on the other hand, they are offered as statements of public opinion or editorial views, many neutrals will accept them, so long as the purpose is understood.

Closely related to these materials are articles from professional journals and scholarly research. For example, in recent years public education in the United States has been studied by several prominent groups, and the reports of these studies have been offered in numerous arbitration cases. Normally these documents will be permitted into the record of hearings, but they are likely to be read and understood to apply only to those issues and locations actually studied.

Other Problems of Evidence

There are additional problems with evidence; improperly obtained evidence and the withholding of evidence are particularly serious. Occasionally a party attempts to gain advantage by improperly obtaining evidence. Wire taps, burglaries, and bribes paid agency or union officials have at times been employed. No neutral will permit the introduction of such evidence, but the burden of proof that evidence was improperly obtained rests with the party making the charge.

The willful withholding of evidence is also unacceptable in arbitration hearings. Evidence that has been withheld from the opposing party will almost always be ruled inadmissible. Moreover, depending upon the evidence, the neutral may even remand the case back to the parties to negotiate in light of the new evidence.

IMPLICATIONS FOR CASE PREPARATION

A great deal has already been presented concerning the implications of procedure for case preparation; however, they are of such critical importance that they must be explicitly addressed.

The rules of procedure, while informal, are sufficiently rigid to assure both parties a fair and equal opportunity to be heard. Legal maneuvering and reliance on technical compliance will rarely form the basis for a favorable arbitration award. Substance of a case's merits is what impresses arbitrators. It is an exceedingly high-risk venture to rely on a technical failure in the procedure without the evidence necessary to prove a claim of harm being inflicted to contractual rights.

Too often, even with the appropriate evidence, advocates do not get everything they could out of documents or testimony. Virtually all courtroom rules of evidence and procedure have a sound substantive basis. For example, laying a foundation for the introduction of evidence can require hours of preparatory investigations and interviews. As a result, advocates sometimes overlook this important aspect of procedure; after all, arbitration is an informal process. However, if the arbitrator is not provided with a proper foundation, how can he or she be expected to know how a document came into existence, or how a witness came to know about certain events? Clearly, the reliability and weight that evidence is assigned depends critically on proper preparation and presentation.

CONCLUSION

The procedure employed in arbitration is similar to that in the courtroom, but is generally less formal. The rules of procedure and evidence govern the manner and type of evidence that can be placed before the neutral. It is therefore critical that the advocate master these rules and procedures. Less direct and maybe even more important, the grievance committeeperson or steward must be aware of the rules of evidence during his or her investigation of a grievance so that important admissible evidence is not ignored in favor of inadmissible evidence.

NOTES

1. See Owen Fairweather, *Practices and Procedures in Labor Arbitration*, 2d ed. Washington, D.C.: Bureau of National Affairs, 1983.

2. For further discussion of these issues in general, see: ibid.

3. See the Code of Ethics of the National Academy of Arbitrators, American Arbitration Association and Federal Mediation and Conciliation Service, Appendix 2.

4. David A. Dilts, "Award Clarification: An Ethical Dilemma?" *Labor Law Journal* 33 (1982): 366–70.

5. See the Voluntary Labor Arbitration Rules of the American Arbitration Association for some general guidelines on how arbitrators will typically handle many of these issues.

6. Arbitrator's award at 71 LA 1238, 1241.

The Arbitration of Contract Interpretation Matters

This chapter and the one to follow focus on the determination of specific merits of general categories of arbitration cases. This chapter is concerned with claims of contract violations other than provisions dealing with disciplinary actions. The next chapter is concerned with disciplinary matters.

Contract interpretation matters are those cases involving the respective rights of the parties outside the disciplinary arena. Such issues as seniority rights for promotions, layoffs, recalls, production standards, and anything involving the guarantees contained in the contract or rights residual to or assigned to management are contract cases.

An examination of this group of cases, issue-by-issue, would take volumes and is clearly beyond the scope of this work. Fortunately, however, there are basic rules of contract interpretation that apply to virtually all cases within this category, therefore, the basic decision-making rules for contract interpretation will be reviewed in this chapter. There are three major rules to the interpretation of a labor agreement: the residual principle, parole rules, and jurisdictional construction principle. Each of these will be reviewed following the discussion of decision making in contract interpretation cases. Then, there is a discussion of minor contract interpretation rules. Finally, a third broad category of cases—whether a particular case is properly before an arbitrator—will be examined.

GENERAL CONTRACT INTERPRETATION

There is another interesting parallel between the courts and arbitration—the decision-making rules. This is nowhere more evident than in arbitral thought concerning the interpretation and application of contract language. There are, however, limitations and complications in applying judicial thought to contract interpretation matters in arbitration, and these must be discussed prior to examining specific decision-making rules.

There are numerous controversies concerning the standards an arbitrator must use in interpreting and applying contract language. In the public sector some of these controversies take on added significance. The two controversies of greatest significance are the nature of the parties' agreement and the role of external law in arbitral decision making.

Nature of the Parties' Agreement

Most labor agreements in both the public and private sectors contain language in the grievance-arbitration clause limiting the arbitrator's authority. Normally an arbitrator is limited to interpreting and applying the totality of the parties' agreement. A narrow arbitration clause proscribes the arbitrator from adding to, subtracting from, or in any way modifying the parties' agreement. In fact, the courts have consistently held, both in the public and private sectors, that an arbitrator must base his or her decision on the essence of the agreement negotiated between the parties. This takes on special significance in most public sector arenas because appeal to the courts is generally more common than it is in the private sector.[1]

If an arbitrator exceeds the authority granted him or her by the parties, the courts will generally set aside the award.[2] An arbitrator's discretion is typically only that granted him or her by the parties, and if the arbitrator exceeds that grant of authority, he or she usurps the parties' rights to freedom of contract.[3] There are those arbitrators and advocates, however, who believe that without discretion an arbitrator cannot serve the best interests of the parties, but that this discretion must be limited to reasonable bounds.

Role of External Law

There is also considerable debate concerning the role of external law in arbitral decision making. The arguments concerning external law are very simple: Some contend that external law, even if not explicitly recognized by the contract, is at least implicitly recognized and must be applied.

However, some advocates and arbitrators believe that unless external law is specifically incorporated or recognized in the labor agreement, an arbitrator is without authority to apply it. The application of external law must be viewed within the context of each specific case. Clearly, an arbitrator's award is subject to judicial review if the award contravenes public policy.

In the private sector, where deferral of administrative law agencies' jurisdiction is common, the role of external law in arbitral decision making presents obvious and serious practical problems.[4] In the public sector, on both state and federal levels, the role external law plays is less directly observable. For example, the scope of bargaining varies substantially from one jurisdiction to another. In one state teacher evaluation criteria are mandatory issues of bargaining, while in a bordering state only evaluation procedures may be negotiated, and the criteria are reserved by statute to the school board. If the school board negotiates procedures that affect criteria in the latter state, then grievances concerning the procedure necessarily involve external law.

It is also not uncommon for public sector contracts to explicitly require the parties to honor state law and to give employees the right to grieve concerning misinterpretations or misapplications of the law. Again, this brings external law directly into the arbitration process. When external law creeps into the arbitration process so does precedent and the attendant problems of decision making, resulting in less efficiency and greater expense in resolving disputes through arbitration. On the other hand, external law may also bring greater predictability to awards in certain cases.

DECISION-MAKING RULES

As was true of procedure, the decision-making rules for contract interpretation cases are borrowed from jurisprudence and adapted to fit the specific needs of parties to collective bargaining, but, in general, they are recognizable to jurists. As was also true of arbitral procedure, quasi-judicial decision-making rules are used to provide predictability and some degree of consistency in arbitral decisions. Predictability, in turn, increases the utility of the arbitration process to the parties.

Residual Principle

The *residual principle* means that anything regarding the operation of the agency or business not specifically given the union by the contract or statute remains a right of management. One of the more common examples of the application of this principle involves promotions. A contract requires that the most senior employee qualified to do the work shall be promoted. The contract explains how seniority for promotion is acquired and how it may be used, but it remains silent on how qualifications are determined. In such a case, as long as the determination of qualifications is not clearly arbitrary, management is free to consider whatever legitimate factors it wishes. It is also interesting to note that the residual principle also applies to union rights. In a recent case, the Oil, Chemical and Atomic Workers filed a grievance in Kansas City concerning management actions in Indianapolis, Tulsa, and Dallas. Management challenged the arbitrability of that grievance since it was not filed at the sites where the violations allegedly occurred. The contract was silent on the issue of where grievances must be filed. The arbitrator reasoned that since the filing of grievances is a union right, the contract's silence on the matter gave the union complete freedom to decide for itself where to file a grievance.

Arbitrators generally believe that the residual principle is limited by several things: Past practice may establish unwritten contract, and, to the extent that it does, imposes a limitation on the application of the residual principle. Statutory law and public policy also place rights with specific parties outside of the four corners of the contract. To the extent that external law applies to a collective bargaining agreement, it also imposes a limitation on the residual principle. These issues are also closely related to the concepts embodied in both the parole rules and jurisdictional construction principle to be discussed below.

Parole Rules

The *parole rules* of evidence dictate to the arbitrator what evidence must be considered first. In general, the best evidence is the most credible and can therefore be heavily weighted. *Best evidence* is that which is admissible in a court; firsthand eyewitness accounts, original documents, expert testimony, and independent observation are best evidence because they are clearly more objective, not subject to interpretation by the witness, and not obviously biased. Hearsay, copies of notes and documents, and testimony known to be biased are not best evidence. The qualitative aspects of the evidence are outside the parole rules of evidence but are necessary to understanding the rules. Evidence—not only its quality but also its source—is the focal point of the parole rules.

The arbitrator must look within the parole rules of evidence for a basis for his or her decision. The parole rules provide the priorities. This ordinal scale is:

1. Clear and unambiguous contract language
2. Past practices and customs
3. Bargaining history
4. Evidence outside of the contract.

In other words, if there is clear and unambiguous contract language, freely negotiated and relied upon by the parties, the arbitrator is obligated to stop at this point and base his or her award on it. There is a not uncommon exception to this: the use of past practice to amend the contract. Remember, the parties must have relied upon the contract's clear language. If the parties have an established practice in contravention to the clear language, the practice will be sustained if mutually understood and relied upon.

If ambiguity exists in the contract language, or if there is no language relevant to the issue, the next step is to examine the record for past practice. The term *past practice* has clear and specific meaning. For an action to attain the status of past practice, and hence become part of the contract, it must meet the following standards:

1. It must be a consistent and frequently used interpretation or method of doing things.
2. It must be clearly understood by both parties.
3. It must be relied upon by both parties.

What does this mean? For example, if management decides to permit employees to eat lunch outside of the plant, and if the employees avail themselves of this opportunity and clearly rely upon it as a right, even though the work rules say they must remain within the plant during their shift, eating outside becomes part of the contract. On the other hand, if an employee is excused from work without pay because of a family reunion, this may not establish a right to leave without pay. If there was only one such incident that was not common knowledge, not relied upon by other employees, and not intended to establish such a right, then no past practice is established.

There are no clear lines by which to judge frequency, reliance, or mutual understanding. Clearly, one incident will not establish a past practice, but do two or three? Or does it take twenty or thirty? Does objecting to a decision prevent the establishment of mutual understanding and reliance? Does placing a bargaining demand on the table to put in the contract clear language contrary to an established practice show a lack of acceptance? There are significant problems with these questions, and they must be viewed within the context of the circumstances and events in specific arbitration cases. There are no clear rules governing decisions on these issues, and many of these controversies are viewed differently by different arbitrators. It should therefore be clear that, to determine whether a past practice has developed, each case must be judged on its relative merits.

Past practice may be used for several purposes: to amend a contract, to fill gaps within a contract, to clarify ambiguous contract language, and to establish new contractual areas.

To amend a contract means that the past practice will substitute for the written language of the contract, or even a previous past practice. Parties frequently find their situation changed, or that the language does not accomplish what was intended. Often the practice evolves over a substantial period of time to correct this difficulty, and it is not uncommon for the practice to remain outside the four corners of the written agreement. That is, the practice is not committed in writing and substituted for the inoperable language. The parties to a contract are often well advised to amend the written language of the contract to reflect its true intent, thus avoiding conflicting practices and language that will almost certainly give rise to disputes.

Using past practice to fill gaps in a contract is to provide guidance in handling elements of actions clearly intended to be covered by the contract but not committed in writing. Frequently the parties fail to contemplate all possible applications of language, and the practice is necessary to govern these gaps. For example, a seniority clause may remain silent on whether temporary supervisors promoted from within the bargaining unit earn seniority while filling the supervisory position. If management continues to count such service for competitive seniority purposes, and the union does not object, the evolved practice provides guidance where the contract has left a gap.

To clarify ambiguous language is to give meaning to unclear language or provide meaning in a specific application. Without past practice attaining contractual status, ambiguous language would present major difficulties, not only for the parties, but also for arbitrators. It is impossible to contemplate all applications of a contract, and what would normally be clear may become ambiguous in a rare application. If practices have developed concerning these rare occurrences, then it may be better to leave the practice in place rather than burden the contract with hundreds of pages that are applicable only on rare occasions. Even here, memorandums, agreements, or letters of understanding are probably still preferable. When ambiguous language is negotiated, the parties' past practices demonstrate how that language is to be read.

Finally, a past practice can simply be a portion of the contract not committed in writing. Established past practices are contractually binding, and some parties have chosen, for whatever reason, not to commit all of these understandings to writing. This adds uncertainty to respective rights, but if the technology or work environment is very dynamic there may be good reason for allowing the practice to remain unwritten.

In cases where competing past practices have developed, or where there is no clear practice or clear language, but intent is shown to have incorporated the issue into the contract, the arbitrator must look to the evidence concerning the parties' bargaining history. Transcripts of negotiations sessions, past contracts, grievances, and testimony from negotiators will often provide insight into what was intended by the parties. By this step in the parole rules, it is too often discovered that the parties may not have had a meeting of the minds concerning a particular issue. It is common for a union negotiator to have one recollection of the bargaining session and the management negotiator to have another. If no such evidence providing insight into the nature of the meeting of the minds is available, then evidence from outside the contract may be considered.

Evidence outside the contract is rarely available, and when it is, it almost always concerns external law. Antidiscrimination statutes, various state bargaining statutes, or the Fair Labor Standard Act may be relied upon to establish rights never mentioned in the contract. When external law is relied upon and noticed by the parties in their negotiations, arbitrators will generally find it binding.

The parole rules give some predictability to how arbitrators will view certain arguments and evidence. Even those arbitrators not legalistically oriented will rely upon the parole rules when faced with issues such as past practice and ambiguous language. The basic contribution of this rule to arbitral decision making is that the arbitrator must rely upon the mutual intent of the parties and must do what is necessary to determine that intent. Further, the arbitrator must also look to the clearest reflection of that mutual intent before moving on to less certain evidentiary grounds. This principle is embodied in those contracts containing narrow arbitration clauses, which require the arbitrator to apply without modification the parties' intent, not his or her own brand of justice.

Jurisdictional Construction Principle

An arbitrator derives his or her authority from the parties and their contract. The arbitrator has no jurisdiction over anything until it is bestowed by the parties to a dispute. This means that the arbitrator is the employee of the union and management, equally and mutually, in one sense: he or she is obligated to the parties and, specifically, the intent of the parties as demonstrated by their contract.

The *jurisdictional construction principle* states simply that the arbitrator's decision must draw its essence from the parties' contract and must be based upon the record of evidence made before the arbitrator. This precludes the arbitrator from administering his or her own personal brand of justice, but the parties' mutual view of justice. This should come as no surprise; it is the intent of most parties when they negotiate an arbitration clause. The institution of arbitration would quickly become unserviceable if the parties' negotiated contract was ignored in favor of some neutral's own personal value system.

The authors have had several cases in which they were convinced both parties were wrong. Even so, that is not for the arbitrator to decide; the arbitrator decides if the contract has been violated. The decision the arbitrator is paid to write is the one that embodies the agreement of the parties. In a recent case, the parties negotiated a seniority clause requiring that "the senior most qualified employee" be promoted. There was a narrow arbitration clause, and the arbitrator was prohibited from adding to the contract. The problem was that the parties failed to put a comma in the seniority clause. Management intended the language to mean "senior, most qualified," but the union intended "senior most, qualified." The arbitrator can do only what the contract intended, in this case, remand the dispute to the parties so that they could have a meeting of the minds. If an arbitrator exceeds his or her jurisdiction or does not draw the essence of the decision from the parties' contract, then the award can the overturned by the courts.[5]

There is another important implication of the jurisdictional construction principle: where there is no agreement or contract, then the grievance, under a narrow clause, is not arbitrable. To find otherwise is, again, for the arbitrator to exceed his or her jurisdiction. On the other hand, if the parties have intended that a neutral would settle disputes, even in the absence of a clear expression of mutual intent, the contract would contain a broad arbitration clause not limiting the arbitrator's authority.

A Synthesis

It is not readily apparent that these rules of contract interpretation are consistent with one another. Some explanation is therefore in order. The jurisdictional construction principle is the beginning point. This principle establishes the arbitrator's authority and, if there is clear language relied upon by the parties, that the decision must be based on that language. If an ambiguity develops or if the contract is one of past practice, then the parole rules of evidence provide the answer. If no evidence can be found within the record of the case in support of one of the parole standards, then the residual principle is the standard of last resort.

The logic in this jurisprudential system is compelling and one of the few things uniformly accepted by arbitrators. For arbitrators to fail in their obligation to adhere to these standards would leave arbitration to the caprice of the individuals who serve as arbitrators, and this result is not intended by the parties or acceptable to the courts.

Precedent

There are two more rules deserving of attention. These are *res judicata* and *stare decisis*. Res judicata is a Latin term meaning "once adjudicated," or "once decided." Stare decisis is also a Latin term, meaning "as decided before." These two decision-making rules are again borrowed from jurisprudence. Res judicata is applied in the same manner as in the courts, but stare decisis is not.

Res judicata requires that if a case has already been adjudicated it may not be tried again, assuming a fair and proper original hearing. In other words, if a losing party is dissatisfied with the result in arbitration, it cannot take the same action based on the previous event and gain another day in court. In an early case, a school board discharged a teacher for incompetence. The case went to arbitration and an arbitrator found the discharge to lack just cause. The employee was reinstated with full back pay and benefits. On his first day back at work, the teacher was discharged again. The discharge notice listed all of the charges contained in the first notice, and his tardiness of five minutes was added to the list. The union again appealed, and the second arbitrator found no significant difference in the charges presented to him and those the teacher was cleared of in the first hearing. The second arbitrator applied res judicata and ordered reinstatement with back pay. Without this rule, a case could be relitigated until a party received the result it desired.

Stare decisis is a rule requiring judges to rely upon precedent in issuing their decisions. No such rule exists for an arbitrator. An arbitrator may take notice of prior decisions in cases similar to the one presently before her or him, but the arbitrator is not bound to base his or her decision on the reasoning of other neutrals. It is the opinion and decision of the arbitrator selected by the parties, and for an arbitrator to be bound by previous decisions circumvents the intent of the parties. Further, law by precedent substantially complicates the arbitration process and may, in fact, defeat the purpose. If precedent were binding, an error in the application of a precedent or the existence of competing precedents would certainly be grounds for appeal, hence turning the arbitration process into a courtroom, which serves nobody save perhaps the arbitrators themselves.

Maybe more importantly, each collective bargaining relationship and the environment in which it has developed has unique elements. If an arbitrator were bound by precedent, dispute resolution through arbitration would become much more complex. An arbitrator would be required to have a record of evidence that would permit a determination of whether previously decided cases were governed by similar language and whether the previous disputes grew out of similar circumstances and facts. This strict adherence to stare decisis would substantially reduce the usefulness of arbitration.

It is interesting to note, however, that arbitrators will pay close attention to how their colleagues have ruled in similar cases. Arbitrators will look for well-established precedents to give credibility to their decisions and the arbitration process, where possible. This is not to say that arbitrators will always apply precedent even though they are not required to do so. Arbitrators apply precedent when the facts clearly indicate the precedent is applicable and consistent with the record of evidence in the case at bar.

ARBITRABILITY

Arbitrability issues are of two types: substantive arbitrability (issues specifically excluded from or simply not included in the contract) and procedural arbitrability (a failure to abide by the rules governing the filing and processing of complaints).

Substantive arbitrability focuses on whether an issue is covered by some provision of the contract and therefore subject to the grievance-arbitration process. By definition, such matters involve the interpretation and application of the labor agreement. Procedural arbitrability, which also involves the interpretation and application of the contract, focuses on whether the grievance was answered, and the answer appealed to the next step in a timely fashion. There are other matters that creep into both categories. For example, if the contract says that employees who have not served their probationary period are not entitled to file a grievance, the alleged violation of a contract effecting only probationary employees may be defended as being nonarbitrable.[6]

Substantive Arbitrability

It is not uncommon for contracts to remain silent on specific issues. The silence of the written agreement is strong evidence of the parties' mutual intent to leave matters concerning this issue to the discretion of management.[7] However, as the discussion concerning the parole rules of evidence demonstrates, this is not so simple. If past practices develop concerning an issue, the parties may have struck a bargain and the issue may be arbitrable.[8]

Often the union and management will agree that certain issues ought not be covered by the contract. Specific exemption from the grievance machinery is also common for certain issues. For example, the U.S. Postal Service and the National Association of Letter Carriers specifically exempt verbal warnings from the grievance procedure. Whatever the logic behind such exemptions, if there is clear language exempting a specific issue from the grievance procedure, it will generally be found to be nonarbitrable.

Procedural Arbitrability

Procedural arbitrability involves the parties' mutual obligation to make the grievance procedure function in a prompt and fair manner. If a grievance is not filed in a timely manner, arbitrators will often find the matter nonarbitrable.[9] The major exception to this rule is if the grievance protests management actions of a recurring nature.[10] In cases of recurring contract violations the union may file at any point, unless the management violations become accepted as a past practice, thereby amending the contract.[11] There is a danger in this class of issues. A consistent failure to protest a management action may result in the union losing a negotiated right. While it is in the best interests of both parties to act responsibly and be accommodative when possible, this desire for a mature bargaining relation must be tempered by the realization that rights can be forfeited by a failure to enforce them.

Employers are sometimes deemed to have lost their right to the contract if they default on their obligation to respond to a grievance or an appeal from lower steps in the grievance procedure in a timely fashion.[12]

Arbitrators are often reluctant to resolve a case on a procedural failure.[13] However, in cases where the procedural failure substantively affects the merits of a case or harms the other party, arbitrators will almost always sustain time limit requirements.[14] The underlying principle that form ought not to control substance is normally relied upon in matters where no harm is inflicted by a delay in filing or processing a grievance. Arbitrators differ in their views of procedural arbitrability questions, and little more can be added to the general rules concerning these issues.

CONCLUSION

The rules governing contract interpretation and application provide for a consistent and logical progression of thought in decision making. The purpose of these rules is not only to provide for order in arbitration, but to assure that only the parties' mutual intent prevails in arbitration matters.

The rules for decision making must be applied on a case by case basis and provide, within broad limits, predictability to arbitrators' awards.

Precedent plays a significant role in arbitration, in that a case already decided may not be relitigated. Precedent in the sense that an arbitrator is bound by the decisions of other neutrals is inconsistent with the role and purpose of arbitration and is not what the parties bargained for. Arbitrators will, however, rely on previous decisions that they find applicable and consistent with the facts in the cases before them, but only when those decisions are correct in their own view.

Arbitrability issues generally focus on the interpretation and application of the contract and can generally be classified into two broad categories: substantive arbitrability and procedural arbitrability. Substantive arbitrability is concerned with contractual coverage of the issue, and procedural arbitrability is concerned with time limits and propriety in the filing, answering, and appealing of grievances.

Appendix 1 contains a sample arbitration opinion and award involving the issue of arbitrability. Appendix 4 contains a sample opinion and award involving matters of contract interpretation.

NOTES

1. See, for example, *W. R. Grace & Co. v. Local 759, Rubber Workers* 103 S. Ct. 2177 (1983) in the private sector, *Devine v. White* 711 F.2d 1082 in the federal sector, and *University of Hawaii Professional Association v. University of Hawaii* 659 P.2d 717, 720, 729, and 732 (Hawaii 1983).

2. Ibid.

3. There is considerable controversy within the arbitration profession concerning this specific issue. For example, see: *Arbitration 1988: Emerging Issues for the 1990s*. Proceedings of the 41st Annual Meetings of the National Academy of Arbitrators. Washington, D.C.: Bureau of National Affairs, 1989.

4. *Collyer Insulated Wire*, 192 NLRB 837 (1971).

5. *Speilberg Manufacturing*, 112 NLRB 1080 (1955).

6. *State of Alaska and Alaska Public Employees Association* (Arbitrator Jackson) 75 LA 635.

7. *U.S. Army, Picatinny Arsenal and American Federation of Government Employees, Local 225* (Arbitrator Cull) 58 LA 988.

8. *School Board District No. 1, Butte, Montana and Butte Teachers Association, Local 332* (Arbitrator Jackson) 59 LA 106.

9. See: *State of Delaware, Department of Health and Social Services and American Federation of State, County and Municipal Employees, Council 81, Locals 1832 and 2030* (Arbitrator DiLauro) 87 LA 563 where a union actually filed a grievance and prevailed in its request for a cease and desist order to get the employer to answer grievances in a timely fashion. For a more traditional application of this principle see: *County of Summit, Board of Mental Retardation and Developmental Disabilities and Weaver Teachers Association* (Arbitrator Duda) 87 LA 763.

10. *Saginaw Board of Education and Saginaw Education Association* (Arbitrator Roumell) 62 LA 1258.

11. *Fox Manufacturing Company and United Furniture Workers of America* (Arbitrator Marshall) 47 LA 97.

12. *County of Santa Clara and Service Employees, Local 715* (Arbitrator Koven) 66 LA 957.

13. For example, see: *City of Honolulu and American Federation of Government Employees, Local 152* (Arbitrator Kanbara) 64 LA 155.

14. *Los Angeles County Probation Department and State, County and Municipal Employees, Local 685* (Arbitrator Rothschild) 68 LA 1373.

The Arbitration of Discipline and Discharge Matters

Discharge and discipline cases are common in arbitration. There are several interesting general observations to be made about this category of rights cases. In general, the management rights clause in the labor agreement gives management the right to discipline or discharge, limited only to reasons characterized as just cause. Even when there is no management rights clause, the residual principle of contract interpretation provides for the same result. The residual principle requires that if a right is not granted to the bargaining unit or the union by contract or statute, that right remains the prerogative of management.[1]

It is also equally true that if the contract does not require that just cause be present for discipline, most arbitrators will find that the right to just cause is present unless specifically renounced in the contract.[2] The reason for this interpretation is the existence of the contract itself. The contract provides rights for the bargaining unit, and if discharge can occur for other than just cause, then those rights specified in the contract are without meaning. Frequently an arbitrator will specifically identify the seniority provision of a contract as critical to this view, but in any event the continuing nature of a contract implies the just cause requirement for discharge.

The basic question with disciplinary matters is whether just cause for the discipline exists. The preponderance of these cases focus on whether the grievant committed the alleged offense. Even though most disciplinary matters are factual disputes, it is still necessary to understand the basic principle of just cause. This issue will be addressed before proceeding to other issues, such as the mitigation of penalties and defenses in the face of just cause.

JUST CAUSE FOR DISCIPLINE

Just cause, proper cause, reasonable cause, or cause are interchangeable terms used to describe the concept of having a reason, related to the employer's activities, to properly administer discipline under the collective bargaining agreement. Advocates and arbitrators have wrestled with this concept for decades, and the matter of just cause is well settled. Just cause is more than simply the reason an action is taken. The concept extends to the reasonableness of the penalty assessed and process used to administer it.[3]

Just cause is therefore a much broader concept than whether the accused individual has committed some misconduct or infraction of the rules. The breadth of just cause protects employees from arbitrary or capricious punishment, but it also protects management's right to maintain control of its work force. It must be remembered that employee protection and management control are very frequently competing ideas, and just cause provides the rationale for balancing those respective rights. Virtually all arbitrators employ some test of the just cause standard, which embodies most, if not all, of the seven tests of just cause, identified from the mainstream of the published arbitration cases, that are presented in the following list:[4]

1. Was there adequate warning?
2. Is the conduct related to employment?
3. Was there prior investigation?
4. Is there sufficient evidence to prove the allegation?
5. Is there consistent treatment of offenses and employees?
6. Does the penalty fit the crime?
7. Was the discipline administered evenhandedly?

The answers to these questions, to the extent they are relevant to the case at hand, determine the existence of just cause. Each of these items will be reviewed in the following paragraphs. Before proceeding, however, these tests of just cause are controversial, and not all arbitrators will apply these standards in all cases. They are presented because they provide the range of issues most often addressed in determining whether just cause exists. It must be remembered, however, that some of the standards may not be at issue in a specific case. In the authors' experience, it is rare for all of the standards to apply in any single case.

Adequate Warning

Offenses for which discipline may be imposed can be categorized into two categories, each with two dimensions. The first category is by the seriousness of the offense: crimes in society and moral turpitude, and crimes in industry. The second category is by the nature of the offense: incidental and habitual. Adequate warning is central to but different in each of these categories.[5]

Adequate warning means that the employee should know what is expected and the penalty associated with violations of those expectations. The easiest category to determine is the seriousness of the offense. Crimes in society and moral turpitude do not require rules proscribing such behaviors. Stealing, sexual misconduct, and battery are unacceptable anywhere in society, including the work place. Employers need not warn employees that what society uniformly holds as improper conduct is grounds for discipline.[6] There is, however, disagreement concerning how far this concept extends. For example, in a recent case an employee was discharged by an employer for yelling "Damn it, damn to hell," after hitting himself on the end of the thumb with a hammer. The outburst occurred on the floor of a printing shop, far removed from customers, yet the employer characterized this outburst as moral turpitude deserving of summary discharge. The employer was a church-owned printing plant manufacturing greeting cards, bibles, and Sunday school lesson materials. While the employee's conduct may not be what the church would have hoped for, there is no element of moral turpitude. For moral turpitude to exist, the conduct must be uniformly unacceptable in society, not only to its most moral segments. As should be readily apparent, some judgment is used to determine moral turpitude. An arbitrator must be careful not to substitute his or her judgment for that of management, if management's judgment is reasonable. On the other hand, an arbitrator must determine the reasonableness of any disciplinary action. This again is a difficult balancing act. The church-employer case is a relatively easy example; unfortunately, most cases are not so easy.

Industrial offenses require specific rules proscribing the conduct. Absenteeism, loitering, failure to meet production schedules, insolence, insubordination, and safety violations require rules that clearly warn the employee that such conduct is unacceptable. However, any established rule must be reasonable and directly related to the employer's proper exercise of authority.[7]

Fair or adequate warning also applies to the nature of the offense. Incidental offenses do not require an attempt to correct behavior, but they may be punished for what they are. An habitual offense requires corrective discipline. For example, insubordination is an incidental offense, and discharge may be imposed as a remedy without any attempt to assist the employee to become subordinate. Absenteeism is an habitual offense for which correction is warranted. With absenteeism the traditional corrective disciplinary procedure generally starts with a warning—written or verbal, or sometimes both—then one or more suspensions, and finally discharge. The nature of the work and the requirements a person faces outside the work place must be balanced with the employer's needs. An honest and reasonable attempt to correct the employee's failure must be evident, or an arbitrator will not sustain discharge for an habitual offense.[8] Corrective measures run the range of counseling to, in the extreme, discharge.

Penalties or ranges of penalties must also be specified for habitual and incident offenses, except for crimes and moral turpitude. Without a warning concerning the penalty likely to befall an employee for misconduct it is unlikely an arbitrator will sustain a discharge. Even with lesser penalties, arbitrators generally look unfavorably upon substantive penalties without fair warning.

Is the Conduct Related to the Employment?

The balancing of the employer's needs with those of the employees is also evident in this portion of the just cause standard. The employer, to impose discipline, must demonstrate that the alleged misconduct adversely affects the agency or business.[9] Many actions, like insubordination, absenteeism, and failure to meet production standards, obviously affect an employer's ability to operate efficiently and are therefore the types of conduct normally warranting discipline. Other behaviors, however, are not so easily connected to the employer's business. For example, a male employee who beats his wife may be subjected to discipline in one business but not in another. If the wife beater is a public schoolteacher, parents may have reason to fear for the safety of their children. Regarding public schoolteachers, a connection may be established between the employee's off-duty conduct and his or her worth to the employer. It is doubtful that such connection could be made for a coal miner or steel worker.

On-duty conduct is almost always easier to connect to employment than off-duty conduct. Without a demonstration of an adverse effect on the employer, off-duty conduct will generally not form the basis for discipline.[10]

Was There Prior Investigation?

An investigation to assure that the relevant facts are known is necessary if discipline is to be sustained. Arbitrators will generally not admit evidence into the record of a hearing that was discovered after the discipline was issued. Without complete discovery and fair and reasonable investigation of the facts of an alleged disciplinary infraction, the disciplinary procedure lacks basic fairness.[11] This is not to say that an employer cannot suspend an employee pending an investigation, but to summarily discharge an employee the record must be sufficiently complete to sustain the action when it is taken.

In cases where the alleged misconduct is threatening to the interests of the agency or the health and safety of employees, an alleged offender can be suspended pending investigation of the facts. Such a suspension is normally permitted by arbitrators if there is probable cause to believe that the suspension is necessary to protect people or property, but there must be an investigation during the period of suspension. Evidence discovered during such a suspension is generally admissible in arbitration hearings.

Is There Sufficient Evidence to Prove the Allegation?

The employer bears the burden of proof in disciplinary matters. To discharge this burden of proof the employer must demonstrate with credible evidence that the accused employee committed the offense. A *prima facie* case is one that is proven.[12] If the employer is successful in establishing a prima facie case, the burden of proof switches to the union, which must provide an appropriate defense to either mitigate or overcome the establishment of just cause (discussed later in the chapter).

The standard applied to determine whether a prima facie case is established is referred to as *quantum of proof*, which is not a settled matter in disciplinary cases. Some arbitrators will find that the employer establishes a prima facie case when the preponderance of evidence supports the employer's claim. Other arbitrators impose different standards for different offenses. Some arbitrators will require proof beyond a reasonable doubt for discharge for a criminal act. The theory behind this standard is that discharge for a crime carries a special stigma that may prevent the accused from finding work elsewhere. Others cite the criminal codes, which require such a standard to prove a crime in the courts. Verbal or written warnings are less serious matters. Many arbitrators who apply the beyond a reasonable doubt standard to discharges for crimes will accept a simple preponderance of the evidence to establish just cause for warnings. It is impossible to determine from the available evidence which group of arbitrators constitute the majority.[13]

Is There Consistent Treatment of Offenses and Employees?

This standard is often referred to as disparate treatment and deals with the penalty assessed for misconduct. If two different employees with identical work records are found guilty of the same offense, they should experience the same penalty, if all other things are equal. If different penalties are assessed identical workers for identical offenses, the disciplinary process lacks basic fairness and may be characterized as capricious.

Disparate treatment is a difficult proposition to prove in many cases where it exists. Normally disparate treatment arguments arise only after just cause is demonstrated in all other respects. To prove disparate treatment, it must be shown that substantially different penalties were assessed for different employees under similar circumstances for the same offense.[14]

One of the most common failures in showing disparate treatment is focusing exclusively on the offense committed, without regard for whether the employees were similarly situated and whether the offenses differed in their severity.

In a recent case, a union defended an employee accused of insubordination. The instant grievant was discharged. The present grievant had less than one year of service and a warning letter for excessive absenteeism. His insubordination involved yelling at a supervisor across the work room floor that he "wasn't about to obey the order of some dumb ———— snot-nosed college kid." The grievant then threw his tools in a trash can and stormed into the break room. After almost forty-five minutes in the break room, he was again ordered to perform the same task and he responded with vulgarity and demanded to see his union representative. The grievant then spent the rest of the shift with the union representative, who convinced the employee to do as he was ordered. The task was done during the second shift by someone else, and a discharge notice awaited the employee the next day.

The union found two other personnel records showing thirty-day suspensions for insubordination. These employees were disciplined for the same incident: A foreman asked the employees to work outside of their classification and they politely refused and asked the foreman to consult the labor agreement. The labor agreement afforded no constraint, and the foreman showed them the relevant portions of the contract. The employees persisted in their refusal to perform the work but did not become loud and were even described as being apologetic. The foreman testified that the two employees refused to do the work because of a matter of principle: the man normally assigned to that classification and the only one qualified to do the job was laid-off. The two employees were model employees with over twenty years service. Both also indicated that they understood that they should have obeyed the order then grieved it, but they preferred to stand on principle, even though they understood it could result in discipline. The union's claim of disparate treatment failed.

Does the Penalty Fit the Crime?

Arbitrators will normally apply a reasonableness standard to ascertain whether the penalty is appropriate. For example, an employee who left the office of a state agency with a state-owned pen valued at two dollars in his hip pocket was stopped by security. The employee was subsequently discharged for theft. The pen was not hidden, but in clear view, and the employee claimed he forgot to put the pen back in his desk. The penalty of discharge for this long-service employee with no previous disciplinary record is clearly outside the bounds of reason.

Discipline for absenteeism possesses many such problems. Are four unexcused absences in one month excessive? What about five ten-minute incidents of tardiness in one month? If the rules prohibit excessive absenteeism and allow management to determine what is excessive, then management is only constrained to be reasonable. Most arbitrators would probably answer yes to both questions.

The penalty must be directly proportional to the offense, but there is simply no clear measure of the magnitude of offenses and penalties. There is an element of subjectivity, therefore, and most arbitrators are hesitant to substitute their judgment for that of management unless the penalty is clearly excessive.

Was the Discipline Administered Evenhandedly?

This standard has two major dimensions. The first concerns selective enforcement of the rules. If there is evidence that management selectively enforces the rules, then the disciplinary process lacks basic fairness. There must be consistency in enforcement. If management, for example, went for years without enforcing its attendance policy, it may not, without warning decide to discipline an individual for excessive absenteeism. Management can regain the right to discipline for excessive absenteeism by giving fair warning to all employees of its intent.

Malice or caprice are also characteristics arbitrators will find unacceptable in the disciplinary process. If rules are enforced for one group of employees (production workers or females) but not for another (skilled tradespeople or men), then discipline for the former group will typically be set aside. If there is evidence of malice against a particular employee, arbitrators will typically find this to be a basis for setting aside a penalty or mitigating discipline.

Just cause requires that each of these seven standards be met, if at issue. The employer typically bears the burden to prove that adequate warning was given, that the offense was committed and investigated, and that the penalty fit the crime. Unions may defeat just cause on the basis of lack of evenhandedness, inappropriate penalty, or disparate treatment, but to prevail the union must prove these latter elements are not present as a defense.

A couple of other issues concerning discipline are worthy of discussion. These issues are mitigation of penalties and defenses once just cause is established.

MITIGATION OF PENALTIES

If management is unsuccessful in proving a prima facie case, a remedy is warranted. In virtually all cases where an employee is found innocent of the allegations, he or she is entitled to full back pay and benefits for the period of the wrongful loss of employment. Back pay is based on the concept of "making whole": the grievant's earnings from other employment or unemployment compensation will be deducted from the back pay to which he or she is entitled.

Mitigation of a penalty is a different concept. The facts of the particular case may demonstrate that the penalty management assessed was excessive and must be reduced. This reduction of a penalty, based on the record of evidence, is referred to as *mitigation of a penalty*, which also differs from leniency. *Leniency* is a managerial prerogative. Basically, leniency is nothing more than an employer extending mercy, or another chance, to an employee. Mitigation is for the arbitrator to decide, while leniency can only be granted by management.

Mitigation of a penalty must be within the requirements of the contract and based on the record of evidence. There are contracts that require the arbitrator to sustain the discharge or reject it totally. Such contract language prohibits the mitigation of a penalty, and even where it may be clearly warranted, the arbitrator is left to make an all-or-nothing decision.

There are several reasons why a penalty may be mitigated. The penalty not fitting the crime is probably the most common. In cases where discharge was assessed, but the record clearly shows the penalty was beyond the bounds of reason for the offense, arbitrators will impose a lesser penalty.[15]

There are often *mitigating* circumstances surrounding misconduct. Management may contribute to an act of insubordination by failing to make orders clear and assure they were understood. An employee may be provoked into misconduct, but these issues will be addressed in greater detail in the following section. A mitigating circumstance is any circumstance that legitimately lessens the severity of the grievant's offense. Factors beyond the grievant's control that lessen the severity of the offense are generally weighed against the nature of the offense to determine whether mitigation is warranted. For example, an employee who commits an unsafe act is subject to discipline, but if management failed to provide the correct tools after they were requested by the employees, and if the unsafe act would not have been committed had the proper equipment been supplied, then mitigation is warranted.

An employee's long and faithful service may also serve to mitigate a penalty. A long-service employee without prior record of discipline is unlikely to repeat an offense and is a better risk for continued good service than a short-service employee with a record of prior discipline. Arbitrators consider such factors together with the nature and severity of the offense to determine whether mitigation is in order. For example, a thirty-year employee progresses through the steps of progressive discipline for excessive absenteeism. The employee, who is going through a contested divorce, was rarely absent more than once a year during his previous twenty-nine years of service. Such a record would be given weight as a mitigating factor, especially if the employee's prognosis for a return to his previous attendance pattern is good.

Arbitrators do differ on the application of mitigation. Many are very hesitant to mitigate penalties, especially in cases where management has considered but rejected the mitigating factors before deciding to impose discipline. Others routinely disturb penalties if mitigating factors are present. The mitigation of penalties is therefore far from a settled issue in the arbitration of disciplinary matters.

DEFENSES IN THE FACE OF JUST CAUSE

Several defenses can serve to overcome just cause for discipline. The most widely cited is the employee's absolute right to refuse an order to do something illegal, immoral, or obviously threatening to his or her health and safety. All a union must do in such an insubordination case is demonstrate this. For example, an employee was recently ordered to remove, without proper protective equipment, insulation containing asbestos from a room. The employee was fired for insubordination; the union demonstrated that the insulation contained asbestos and that the employee was denied protective equipment. The grievant was insubordinate, but his insubordination was not just cause for discipline.

Discipline for brawling is rather common. Often company or agency rules specify discharge for anyone participating in a brawl, aggressor not. A proper defense for brawling is self-defense, which must be against an aggressor using force not in excess of that necessary to defend one's self. This defense, however, assumes that the grievant did not provoke the attack.

Absenteeism generates some interesting defenses. An employee injured for an accident compensable under workmen's compensation may generally not be disciplined for his or her absenteeism, generally a statutory right established in the workmen's compensation law. The proper and successful defense would be to demonstrate that the absences were due to the compensable injury.

To the extent that an employer contributes to an employee's misconduct, there is an available defense. For example, an employee is disciplined for not meeting production standards on a job she recently bid into. The employee met standards for her first three weeks and was permanently awarded the job. During her fourth week the agency installed new switches on the machine she operated that required, according to the industrial engineers, two more seconds to cycle the machine. This additional time was accounted for in her production rate, but she consistently failed to meet her rate for the next two weeks. She received a written warning, which she grieved. She claimed that not only did the machine take longer to cycle, but the new switches were complicated and she did not understand how everything worked. The evidence showed the machine's switches to be quite complex, much more so than the previous machine. The agency failed to provide any training, and even her foreman, who had formerly held the grievant's job, testified he had no idea how to operate the new machine. Clearly, management contributed to the grievant's failure to meet standards, and the union's defense prevailed.

There are numerous such defenses, each based on the grievant not being culpable of the apparent misconduct, or management's failure substantially contributing to the employee's offense. For example, if a grievant was provoked into name calling by a supervisor, discipline will probably not be sustained. Discipline for off-duty conduct is also rather common, but for an arbitrator to sustain a disciplinary penalty the employer must show a substantial interest in the employee's conduct and that the employer is affected by the conduct.[16]

CONCLUSION

Discharge and discipline are based on the multifaceted concept of just cause, which requires that an offense adversely affects the employer, and that the procedures used to discipline must be fair and reasonable. Just cause also requires that the penalty fit the crime. Even if just cause is demonstrated, mitigation is often possible if the record of evidence so demonstrates.

Numerous defenses can be erected to protect a wrongfully accused grievant. It falls upon the union to disprove misconduct.

A word of warning is in order. Too often unions use the "shotgun" approach for disciplinary grievances. That is, the union may try to discredit the company's just cause case, proceed to erect four or five defenses, and then argue that three different mitigating circumstances exist. Such an approach frequently results in a couple of obviously meritless attempts to have the discipline set aside and makes other elements of the case suspect. Union advocates should not proffer arguments and defenses simply to muddy the waters, hoping the arbitrator will become confused and award in their favor. Too often such strategies backfire.

Appendix 5 contains a sample arbitration opinion and award involving disciplinary matters.

NOTES

1. *Springfield Board of Education and Springfield Local of Association of Classroom Teachers* (Arbitrator Feldman) 87 LA 16.

2. *City of St. Petersburg and International Brotherhood of Firemen and Oilers, Local 1220* (Arbitrator Vause) 87 LA 673.

3. *San Francisco Public Utilities Commission and Transport Workers, Local 250A* (Arbitrator Eaton) 61 LA 1047.

4. BNA Editorial Staff, *Grievance Guide*. Washington, D.C.: Bureau of National Affairs, 1978, pp. 1–3.

5. *Alabama Department of Mental Health and Laborers, Local 1279* (Arbitrator Spritzer) 66 LA 279.

6. *City of Compton, Fire Department and Firefighters, Local 2216* (Arbitrator Rule) 65 LA 1115.

7. *City of Janesville and State, County and Municipal Employees, Local 523* (Arbitrator Schurke) 64 LA 783.

8. *City of Flint and Firefighters, Local 352* (Arbitrator Stieber) 59 LA 370.

9. *Veteran's Administration Medical Center and American Federation of Government Employees, Local 547* (Arbitrator Sherman) 55 LA 92.

10. Ibid.

11. *Warren Board of Education and Warren Teachers Association* (Arbitrator Mittenthal) 50 LA 812.

12. *City of Hartford and Police Local 308* (Connecticut State Board) 62 LA 1281.

13. *Michigan Department of State Police and Municipal Employees, Local 1034* (Arbitrator Borland) 87 LA 59.

14. Owen Fairweather, *Practices and Procedures in Labor Arbitration*, 2d ed. Washington, D.C.: Bureau of National Affairs, 1983, pp. 503–04.

15. *Social Security Administration and American Federation of Government Employees, Local 1395* (Arbitrator Wolff) 87 LA 1026.

16. *Regional Transportation District and Amalgamated Transit Union 1001* (Arbitrator Vernon) 87 LA 793.

8

Decision Making and Arbitrators

This chapter treats arbitrator decision making. First, available published research is examined for the light it sheds on who arbitrators are and the role they play in the parties' disputes. Next, the authors draw upon their own experiences for additional insight on this topic as well as what prospective arbitrators might expect as members of the profession.

The previous chapter examines the specific standards applied by arbitrators in specific types of cases. Arbitration, however, includes more than fixed standards. Arbitrators are human beings and as a result bring personal characteristics to their work. As has been said repeatedly throughout this book, arbitrators are selected by the parties through a market mechanism, and, therefore, successful arbitrators are generally well versed in their trade and have personal characteristics the parties, in aggregate, find acceptable. Even so, some remarks about arbitrators and their decision-making processes are in order.

ARBITRATORS: WHO THEY ARE AND WHAT THEY DO

Arbitrators are, for the most part, professional neutrals who have gained the trust of both unions and management. Arbitrators serve two conflicting masters equally, and the expressed will of the arbitrators' employers is to be found in their collective bargaining agreements. In one sense, arbitrators are nothing more than "creatures of the contract." It is through the parties' grievance procedure or submission agreement that the arbitrator is called to decide a specific dispute. Unlike judges, arbitrators are not appointed or elected by persons not directly involved in the controversy. Arbitrators are selected by the parties whom they serve, and even those arbitrators that serve as permanent umpires can be dismissed should the parties believe it is in their mutual interest to do so. This market mechanism serves to provide the parties with arbitrators that have proven themselves. However, the field of arbitration has changed over the years and is being expanded and refined, requiring arbitrators to remain current with the field and the parties' needs.

In recent years the role of labor arbitrators has been expanded to include the interpretation and application of external law.[1] There have also been substantial experiments in dispute resolution that rely heavily on arbitrators to mediate grievance disputes.[2] Like any other social or legal institution, arbitration is dynamic. The dynamics of the field also change the role arbitrators play in labor-management relations.

In many important respects the role of arbitrator has changed over time; however, the central role of the arbitrator—to provide two parties with a neutral third-party decision in disputes concerning the interpretation and application of their contract—has remained very stable. The contract evolves and the role that external law plays in a contractual relationship changes, but the contract governs the parties' behavior and determines what role the arbitrator can serve. Therefore, to the extent that collective bargaining is a dynamic process and that the legal environment changes, the roles arbitrators are asked to play also change.

Most successful arbitrators bring considerable expertise and experience to most arbitration cases. However, many are relatively new to the profession. Recent studies show that there is very little difference in the decisions of arbitrators once they have some threshold of experience—about twenty cases.[3] In recent years there has been considerable academic research concerning arbitrators' decisions and whether demographic or other measurable characteristics influence arbitral thought.[4] There has also been research concerning the quality of representation and how it affects the probability of prevailing in specific cases.[5] The research, to date, is inconclusive about the effects of demographics on arbitral decision making. A few generalizations can, however, be offered. It appears that experience, to a point, is an important determinant of the quality of arbitration services. Experience is also a test of acceptability to the parties, because only those arbitrators that have or are gaining party acceptability will attain experience. The available evidence also suggests that there is some support for the idea that education is important in gaining acceptance by the parties. What seems most clear, however, is that parties have more faith in arbitrators they know something about. These common-sense results are consistent with what most experienced advocates have discovered through years of representing labor or management.

There has been considerable discussion about the role and practices of arbitrators. There are several very cogent discussions of the subject in the literature by respected "mainline" arbitrators.[6] Rather than replicate these discussions here, the reader is urged to include these discussions in their must-read list. There are a few key points, however, that deserve attention before proceeding.

Arbitrator Harry Dworkin examines several issues of practical significance. He contends that arbitrators (professional, hence, acceptable ones) are not at all influenced by several factors: personal treatment (flattery or abuse), the possibility of repeat business, and the parties' demeanor during the hearing. This is not to say that the parties can flatter or abuse an arbitrator and expect no reaction. Quite the contrary, most widely acceptable arbitrators would not appreciate either type of behavior and would probably refuse to serve those parties engaging in such behavior.

Dworkin also analyzes the value of briefs and citations. He points out correctly that in most cases the arbitrator has some impression of the merits of the case by the end of the hearing. Posthearing briefs are filed frequently, and they are often lengthy discourses on the merits of the case. Briefs may be of value to the extent that they help organize and clearly state the parties' positions and the evidence presented in the hearing, however, Dworkin also states that it is impossible to offer any generalization about the values of briefs to the decision making of the arbitrator. Citations of precedent, however, are a different matter. Arbitrators, like judges and lawyers, look for "security blankets," and citations of cases involving similar facts and circumstances surrounding similar issues are sometimes of value.

Arbitrator Watt McBrayer offers a philosophical discussion of what an arbitrator is expected to provide the parties. McBrayer raises two critical points: the parties must live with the decision the arbitrator will issue, and that decision should be the one they would have mutually arrived at if given the opportunity to objectively view their own contract and the evidence. In other words, the arbitrator must sustain the mutual intent of the parties as he or she finds it. Further, McBrayer contends that the arbitrator must be fair and exercise good judgment. This extends far beyond the final product, the award, but also includes an awareness that in every case someone feels they have been wronged. The arbitrator must take care to provide adequate and clear reasoning so that the losing party understands why it should not prevail. This does not mean that the arbitrator must provide solace, but substantial and contractually based reasons for his or her decision.

Much has been learned about how arbitrators decide cases, who the neutrals are, and what arbitration's role is in the administration of a contract. There is, however, a great deal yet to be discovered. Arbitrators themselves would have a great deal of difficulty providing solid and enduring generalizations about how they decide cases, not because they are an evasive lot, but because each case has unique characteristics, and the arbitrator is responsible to account for that uniqueness in each decision. The following sections of this chapter overlap what has already been discussed but focuses more on the individual serving as arbitrator than generalizations concerning the profession.

ARBITRATORS AS DECISION MAKERS

There is no magic involved in arbitral thought, or at least there should not be. The arbitrator has no special facilities, save experience, to determine whether someone is lying or being truthful. The arbitrator has no crystal ball in which to gaze to see events, past or future. The arbitrator rarely possesses the wisdom of Solomon. What the arbitrator has is a record of evidence and a collective bargaining agreement. The arbitrator will have the various claims of the parties and must use the evidence and the contract to ascertain what the parties are entitled to have for an award.

Arbitrators are nothing more than triers of fact, and the facts and contentions to be placed before the arbitrator are, for the most part, determined by the union and management representatives who have prepared their respective cases. Labor or management will prevail in or lose a case simply on merit. In fact, recent research has shown that the party bearing the burden of proof will lose in a majority—about 57 percent—of their cases.[7] This illustrates the point that you cannot win a case unless the facts and the contract support your case!

In most respects, advocates find this explanation less than satisfying. They would rather that all arbitrators have special insight into human character or some special trick to determine whose claims are the most legitimate. Satisfying or not, there are simply no special tricks or gimmicks. Arbitrators base their decisions on the magic of the meeting of the minds during contract negotiations and the facts presented during hearings.

Decisions in arbitration cases are based on the record of evidence and determined by the requirements of the parties' contract. Sorting through evidence, rejecting the incredible and accepting the credible, provides the record of evidence. An impartial reading of the contract language and then applying the record of evidence to that language is how the vast preponderance of all arbitration cases are decided.

Arbitrators have relatively wide experience in the types of cases that come before them and have better than average judgment, otherwise they would not be arbitrators. The one thing an arbitrator does have that the parties may lack is impartiality. This lack of a stake in the outcome allows the arbitrator to look objectively for the answer required by the evidence and contract. Very frequently this objectivity is sufficient to give the appearance of something more reasonable, but "what you see is what you get."

THE MARKET AND ARBITRATION

Before the accusation is made that the authors have evaded the issue of decision making it is necessary to understand why the above claims have been made. Most arbitration in the United States is not compulsory, as it is in interest disputes and in Australia. The parties have agreed to be bound by the decision of a neutral third party whom they have selected. The parties to grievances always select the arbitrator, whether a permanent umpire or an arbitrator selected ad hoc. In either case, the parties either agree they have faith in a particular arbitrator, or they have selected the arbitrator by striking the most unacceptable from a list provided by an administrative panel. If arbitrators were not neutrals capable of conducting a hearing and writing a decision based on the record of evidence, the parties would quickly determine that arbitrator to be deficient. The best arbitrators gain wide party acceptability and survive the test of the market, and those who do not gain party acceptability fail and become advocates, judges, or college professors. To say that arbitrators simply weigh the record of evidence and provide an objective determination on the merits of each case is therefore not a tribute to those who enter the profession, but it is a tribute to the market selection process that retains the capable and dismisses the less capable. The market, as economists argue, provides the parties themselves with ultimate control over the process. Arbitrators that provide good service, fair awards based on the contract, and well-reasoned opinions will become acceptable. Those that fail in their basic obligations will not gain party acceptability and hence not be sought out to serve as arbitrators. The market is a fair test and has provided efficient dispute resolution to parties for nearly fifty years.

If there was a magic formula or hidden agenda in arbitration, it would be in this book. Arbitration is nothing more than common sense and gleaning from the parties' agreement and the record of evidence what the best decision is.

CONCLUSION

Arbitral decision making is, as we speak, being subjected to intensive examination. Very little has been uncovered to this point. Decision making and the thought processes of arbitrators do not lend themselves well to empirical examination; however, some progress is being made and we should expect a great deal more in the near future.

The authors believe arbitration has served parties well because those who survive are selected through a market mechanism where the consumer is still the major player. Arbitrators that survive the test of time and market forces are, for the most part, exceptional people whose fairness and judgment have been tested and not found deficient. If Adam Smith's observations in the *Wealth of Nations* have meaning, as the authors believe, the magic in arbitration is the magic of an effective market place culling out the unworthy and offering the worthy.

NOTES

1. See, for example: Richard Mittenthal, "The Role of Law in Arbitration," *Development in American and Foreign Arbitration, Proceedings of the Twenty-first Annual Meeting of the National Academy of Arbitrators*. Washington, D.C.: Bureau of National Affairs, 1968, pp. 42–57.

2. Stephen Goldberg, "Grievance Mediation: A Successful Alternative to Labor Arbitration," *Negotiation Journal: On the Process of Dispute Settlement*, vol. 5, no. 1 (January 1989): 9–15.

3. J. T. Sphere and J. Small, "Members and Nonmembers of the National Academy of Arbitrators: Do They Differ?" *The Arbitration Journal*, vol. 39 (September 1984): 25–33.

4. See: Orley Ashenfelter, "Arbitrator Behavior," *Proceedings of the American Economic Association*, vol. 77 (1987): 342–46; and David Bloom and Christopher Cavanaugh, "An Analysis of the Selection of Arbitrators," *American Economic Review* 76 (1986): 408–22 for discussions of the exchangeability hypothesis in interest arbitration cases.

5. See, for example: Herbert Heneman and Marcus Sandver, "Arbitrators' Backgrounds and Behavior," *Journal of Labor Research*, vol. 4, no. 2 (Spring 1983): 115–24; and N. E. Nelson and E. M. Curry, "Arbitral Decision Making: The Impact of Occupation, Education, Age and Experience," *Industrial Relations*, vol. 20 (1981): 312–17.

6. The most practical, hence useful to the advocate, are: Harry Dworkin, "How Arbitrators Decide Cases," *Labor Law Journal* (April 1974): 200–10 and Watt H. McBrayer, "What Is Expected of an Arbitrator," *The Arbitration Journal*, vol. 9, no. 1 (1954): 37–41.

7. David A. Dilts and Clarence R. Deitsch, "Arbitration Win/Loss Rates as a Measure of Arbitrator Neutrality," *The Arbitration Journal*, vol. 44, no. 3 (September 1989): 42–57.

9

Afterword

This work is the second text in a series concerning collective bargaining in the public sector. The companion volume, David A. Dilts and William J. Walsh, *Collective Bargaining and Impasse Resolution in the Public Sector*, published by Quorum Books in 1988, is concerned with contract negotiations and the resolution of impasses during this stage of bargaining. In some respects contract negotiations have substantially more sex appeal. The plain truth is that the hard and unsung work of collective bargaining occurs during the administration of the agreement hammered out at the bargaining table. To be an effective representative of labor or management, or just a well-informed citizen, the reader must master the principles of both contract negotiations and administration.

In an era that has witnessed the relative decline of the traditionally unionized goods-producing and transportation industries, the public sector is somewhat of an enigma. While unions are in decline in the private sector, they are becoming increasingly important in government employment. Much of what is known of collective bargaining applies to both the public and private sectors. However, there are substantial differences in the economics and technologies of service industries that affect labor-management relations. The difference between service and goods producing industries explains some of the uniqueness of public sector bargaining. The differences in the philosophical, political, and legal environments in which bargaining occurs may be even more important. The legal environment, which reflects the political and philosophical environments, is significantly different in public employment. The economic realities in the public sector also differ substantially from that of the private sector. It should not come as any serious surprise to anyone, then, that public sector collective bargaining differs in many important respects from the negotiations observed in the private sector.

What is perfectly clear from the available evidence is that the nature of impasse resolution, contracts, and grievance administration is significantly different in the public sector. Part of the motivation for writing these volumes is that most of the work presently available to students and practitioners is focused primarily on the private sector or takes a "generic" approach that fails to give an adequate understanding of the needs of parties in either the public or private sectors.

A couple of final thoughts: First, there is a great deal of variation in collective bargaining across the states, and there are substantial differences between the levels of government. We have tried to account for the differences in the nature and requirements of negotiations across jurisdictions. Accounting for wide variations, however, is problematic. If you represent labor or management in New York, you will find that places like Iowa or Kansas have a great number of similarities but are still quite alien. This suggests that comparative studies of states or levels of government must be published for a complete understanding of public sector collective bargaining.

Second, collective bargaining in the public sector is a creature unlike the private sector because of a lack of consistency. Americans are traditionally suspicious of central government, leaving local problems to local authorities. This basic constitutional philosophy has resulted in many states enacting collective bargaining statutes that approximate the protections of the Taft-Hartley Act. On the other hand, some states have virtually outlawed collective bargaining for state and local government employees. This observation has serious implications, not only for the workers within these jurisdictions, but also for public services. The evidence concerning the implications of these differences is incomplete, and few, if any, conclusions can be drawn. In the next decade there will be increasing private sector intrusion into traditional public sector activities accompanied by broader applications of the Taft-Hartley Act. There may even be labor law reform that addresses the needs of public sector employers and employees. Clearly, the next decade will be a dynamic period that will witness the maturing of negotiations in the public sector and probably the birth of collective bargaining in areas where it is now unknown. If the reader is to be prepared for the evolutionary period we are about to enter, he or she must understand where we are now.

The authors hope this text will prove valuable to the reader and, together

with its companion volume, provide the necessary information and knowledge to be an effective representative.

Appendix 1

Rights Arbitration: Arbitrability

ARBITRATION OPINION AND AWARD

(IN RE LOCAL 4407)
(AMERICAN FEDERATION OF)
(PUBLIC EMPLOYEES)
(AFL–CIO)
(AND)
(ARMY ORDNANCE CENTER)
(FMCS CASE NO. 88–17319)
(GRIEVANCE: PRESELECTION)

ARBITRATOR:

DR. CLARENCE R. DEITSCH
MUNCIE, INDIANA
SELECTED BY THE PARTIES
THROUGH THE PROCEDURES
OF THE FEDERAL MEDIATION
AND CONCILIATION SERVICE

DATE OF GRIEVANCE: April 15, 1988 (Step 2 Advance)

DATE OF HEARING: August 1, 1989

DATE OF AWARD: October 1, 1989

Appearances: For the Union: Richard Lewellen, Chief Steward, Local 4407, American Federation of Government Employees. For the Employer: Michael Hamlin, Assistant Counsel, Army Ordnance Center.

IMPROPER PRESELECTION FOR PROMOTION/ PROCEDURAL ARBITRABILITY OF GRIEVANCE

The Issues

DEITSCH, Arbitrator—(1) Was Mr. Carl Lohrey improperly denied training for the Packaging Specialist Position? If so, what should the remedy be? (2) *Threshold* Issue: Did the Union fail to advance the grievance to Step 3 in a timely fashion, thereby terminating (i.e., resolving by default) said grievance?

Stipulated Evidence (Joint Exhibits)

1. *Agreement Between Army Ordnance Center & Local 4407 American Federation of Government Employees, AFL-CIO—Effective 1 January 1987.*
2. Continuation of First Step Grievance Period, dated 27 April 1988.
3. Second Step Grievance Advance, dated 15 April 1988.
4. Response to Second Step Grievance, dated 6 June 1988.
5. Third Step Grievance Advance, dated 9 June 1988.
6. Response to Third Step Grievance, dated 22 June 1988.
7. Fourth Step Grievance Advance, dated 27 June 1988.
8. Notice of Intent to Arbitrate, date 20 July 1988.

Relevant Contract Provisions

Article 36: Grievance Procedure

Section E.   If a grievance is rejected at any step as not grievable under this procedure, the grievance will be considered amended to include the grievability issue. Failure to declare a matter not grievable or discussion of the merits of the grievance at any step shall not constitute a waiver of the right to do so. However, this right to declare a grievance not grievable shall be waived if not asserted in the final AOC or Union decision.

Section H.   A grievance will be considered timely initiated under this procedure only if filed at the proper step of this procedure within 15 calendar days after the matter being grieved occurred, unless another time limit is specifically provided in Sections D or J. If, however, the applicable employee or party could not have been reasonably aware of the occurrence of the matter, the time limit shall begin to run from the time the applicable employee or party could first have been reasonably aware of the occurrence. For this purpose, notice to the employee constitutes notice to the Union. If the party against whom the grievance is filed fails to observe the time limits of this procedure, the aggrieved party may advance the grievance to the next step. *If the aggrieved party fails to meet a time limit, the grievance is automatically terminated.* The time limits of this procedure shall be strictly construed, and a party rejecting a grievance as untimely filed, advanced, or processed shall not be required to show that it would be prejudiced if the grievance were to be permitted to proceed. All time limits may be extended by mutual consent;

an agreement to extend shall be in writing but shall not establish a past practice or waiver with respect to any future expansions. (Emphasis added)

Section I. Procedures for Employee Grievances

(1) STEP 1. Except as otherwise provided in Sections D or J, the grievance will first be taken up orally by the aggrieved employee alone, or with Union representation, with the employee's immediate supervisor in an attempt to settle the matter. If the employee presents a matter directly to AOC for adjustment consistent with the terms of this Agreement, the Union shall be entitled, upon its request, after being notified, to have an observer present when the response is given at the first step, and at all meetings at subsequent steps. The first line supervisor will give his/her response to the grievant within 7 working days after the meeting. If the matter is not satisfactorily resolved at Step 1, the grievance may be advanced to Step 2 within 7 working days after the response at Step 1, or within 14 working days after the initial filing of the grievance if there is no response.

(2) STEP 2. A grievance advanced to Step 2 shall be submitted in writing to the Division Director. It shall generally be signed by the aggrieved party, contain a brief statement of the grievance and indicate the time and place of the meeting at the first step. The Division Director or his/her designee will meet with the grievant and his/her designated representative within 5 working days of the receipt of the grievance, and will give his/her answer within 10 working days thereafter. *If the grievance is not satisfactorily resolved at Step 2, it may be advanced to Step 3 within 5 working days after the response at Step 2* or within 20 working days after filing Step 2 if there is no response. (Emphasis added)

(3) STEP 3. A grievance advanced to Step 3 shall be submitted in writing to the Department Director. It shall be signed by the aggrieved party, contain a clear statement of the grievance (including, as applicable, references to rules, regulations, etc.), a statement of the relief sought, and a statement indicating the time and place of the meeting at the second step. The Department Director or his/her designee will meet with the grievant and his/her designated representative within 5 working days thereafter. If the grievance is not satisfactorily resolved at Step 3, it may be advanced to Step 4 within 10 working days after issuance of the written answer at Step 3, or if no answer is issued, within 20 working days after filing at Step 3.

Article 37: Arbitration

SECTION A.   If a grievance filed under Article 36 is not satisfactorily resolved, either party may submit the matter to arbitration by giving the other party written notification within 30 calendar days after issuance of a final decision.

SECTION B.   If arbitration is invoked, within 5 working days after one party has so notified the other, *the parties shall jointly request the Federal Mediation and Conciliation Service to provide a list of seven impartial persons* qualified to act as an arbitrator. Within 5 working days after the list is received, the parties shall meet and alternately strike one name until only one remains. The person whose name remains will be the selected arbitrator. The parties shall flip a coin to determine which strikes first. (Emphasis added)

SECTION C. In interpreting this Agreement, the arbitrator shall maintain full recognition that the parties are in the Federal Sector of employment, and that established principles in the private sector may not be applicable.

SECTION D. *The arbitrator shall not have the power to add to, subtract from, or otherwise modify the terms of this Agreement or supplementary agreement.* He/she shall have jurisdiction to resolve only the grievance presented, and to grant relief only to the particular grievant. Findings of alternate means of resolution are not authorized. (Emphasis added)

SECTION E. If the parties fail to agree on a joint submission of the issue(s) for arbitration, each shall submit a separate submission and the arbitrator shall determine the issue or issues to be heard.

SECTION F. The arbitrator's and court reporter's fees shall be borne equally by AOC and the Union. *However, if so requested by a party, and where arbitrability and/or grievability is an issue, the arbitrator shall make a finding as to whether a clearly nongrievable or nonarbitrable grievance has been pursued in bad faith. If bad faith on the grievability/arbitrability issue is found, the arbitrator shall assess all such fees to the party advancing the grievance.* Should the moving party elect to forgo arbitration, once an arbitrator is selected, that party shall be responsible for notifying the other in writing and for the payment of any cancellation charges. The arbitration hearing will be held, if possible, on AOC's premises during the regular day shift hours of the basic workweek. Witnesses who are AOC employees shall not suffer loss of pay because of their participation. No more than two persons will be authorized to represent the Union at such hearings. (Emphasis added)

Positions of the Parties Regarding the Threshold Issue of Procedural Arbitrability

The following positions were taken by the Army Ordnance Center (AOC) and Local 4407, American Federation of Public Employees (AFPE), respectively, in a hearing before the Arbitrator on Tuesday, August 1, 1989 at the Army Ordnance Center, 15330 West 7th Street, Cincinnati, Ohio.

Employer:

Article 36, Section H of the *Agreement* (Joint Exhibit #1) mandates the automatic termination of any grievance where the aggrieved party fails to meet a time limit—provided that the time limit has not been extended by mutual consent. In the instant case, the Union failed to advance the grievance to Step 3 within the 5 working days specified by the *Agreement* after having failed to achieve a satisfactory resolution of the grievance at Step 2. Specifically, the Union was advised of the Employer's denial (i.e., given a response) at Step 2 on June 6, 1988 (Joint Exhibit #4), but failed to advance the grievance to Step 3 until June 14, 1988—one working day after the time limit had expired. Consequently, per the *Agreement*, the grievance was "automatically terminated."

Union:

The Employer had an established past practice of ignoring and waiving time limits for the processing of grievances from one step to the next step of the grievance procedure. This disregard of time limits is reflected in the instant case by the Employer's failure to observe the time limits specified in the *Agreement* (i.e., Article 37, Section B) for petitioning the Federal Mediation and Conciliation Service for a panel of arbitrators after having been notified of the Union's intent to arbitrate (Joint Exhibit #8)—waiting approximately a month and a half before petitioning for a panel of arbitrators (Union Exhibit #1)—a period of time far in excess of the five working days specified by Article 37, Section B of the *Agreement*. Lastly, the simple fact of the matter is that the Step 3 Grievance Advance (Joint Exhibit #5) was hand delivered to the Employer on June 9, 1988—within the five working days specified by the *Agreement* for a Step 3 Appeal. Hence, the grievance was processed in a timely fashion and is, therefore, arbitrable.

Discussion and Opinion

Since the Employer raised the threshold issue of procedural arbitrability—that is, since it raised the timeliness issue as an affirmative defense, it bears the burden of proving the truth of the matter affirmed. It will be presumed that the Union met all time limits for grievance processing until the Employer establishes by a "preponderance of the evidence" the contrary.

A. WAIVER OF PROCEDURAL TIME LIMITS

Article 36, Section I, paragraph 2 of the *Agreement* establishes *clear* time limits for appealing a grievance from Step 2 to Step 3, namely, "within 5 working days after the response at Step 2, or within 20 working days after filing at Step 2 if there is no response" (Joint Exhibit #1, p. 33). Equally *clear* is the penalty specified by Article 36, Section H of the *Agreement* for the failure of the *aggrieved party* to meet/observe grievance time limits, namely, that "the grievance is automatically terminated" (Joint Exhibit #1, p. 33).

Although the Union argued that the above-noted time limits had been waived by established past practice, the only evidence supportive thereof were the statements of Witnesses Tammi Ramsey and William Shockley that time limits had been mutually waived in the case of environmental differential pay grievances. That any such waiver of time limits was the exception rather than the rule—that there was no established past practice waiving grievance processing time limits in general—is overwhelmingly established by referencing the *Agreement*, by referencing documentary evidence submitted at the hearing, and by referencing the testimony of the two union witnesses regarding the arbitrability issue.

As for the *Agreement*, Article 36, Section H states:

> The time limits of this procedure shall be *strictly construed*, and a party rejecting a grievance as untimely filed, advanced, or processed shall not be required to show that it would be prejudiced if the grievance were permitted to proceed. All time limits may be extended by mutual consent; an agreement to extend shall be in writing but *shall not establish a past practice* or waiver with respect *to any future extensions*. (Emphasis added)

That the foregoing language was given its literal interpretation by both parties in the instant case is reflected by the memorandum mutually extending "the time limits for responding to the first step grievance and the advancing of any unresolved issues to the second step . . ." entitled "Continuation of First Step Grievance Period" (Joint Exhibit #2). This document concludes, in pertinent part:

After issuance of the final decisions at the first step, the remaining steps, if any, of the grievance *will follow the time limits established . . . unless otherwise covered by separate memorandum.* (Emphasis added)

A separate memorandum was not entered during the arbitration hearing.

The testimony of the Union's two witnesses, Tammi Ramsey and William Shockley, also indicates that grievance processing time limits were being strictly enforced. Under direct examination in response to the question of whether she knew anything specifically about the processing of the instant grievance from Step 2 to Step 3, Ms. Ramsey responded:

Anything specifically? About the only thing I know for sure is that I think we were running close on time. And I believe, in fact, I'm almost sure that you (Lewellen) came to me and told me that we had to get this processed. We had conversation about that and you didn't have the time to take that letter up. And I was busy that day. And you wanted Bill Shockley to run that letter upstairs for you. And I, from what you told me, you'd gotten a hold of Bill Shockley and he . . .

Mr. Shockley confirmed the urgency of prompt delivery to make the Step 3 filing deadline and thereby avoid any question of timeliness by testifying that Mr. Richard Lewellen directed him to hand deliver the Step 3 Appeal to Department Director Carl Shoecraft's office before the close of business on June 9, 1988. According to Mr. Shockley, he had delivered the Step 3 Grievance Appeal (Joint Exhibit #5) to Labor Relations Specialist Charlotte Shelley and secured a receipted copy of same, because Department Director Shoecraft's substitute secretary ("I think her name is Betty") refused to provide such a receipt indicating that the filing deadline had been met.

Not only does the foregoing testimony indicate that grievance processing limits were being stringently enforced and that the Union was aware of this fact, but it also indicates that the Union clearly understood the manner in which said deadlines had to be met. Stated somewhat differently, the Union clearly understood that appeals of employer responses at the various steps of the grievance procedure had to be in the *physical possession* of designated managerial personnel within the contractually specified time limits after denial of the grievance at the previous step. At no time did the Union claim or contend that depositing an appeal/advancement either in the U.S. or AOC mail within the contractually specified time limits satisfied those requirements. Indeed, the statements of the Union witnesses establishing the need for and alleging actual delivery of the Step 3 Appeal constitute *prima facie* evidence that deposit of said appeal in the U.S. or AOC mail did not meet the contractual time limits.

The Union's argument that the Employer's disregard/violation of the time limit specified by Article 37, Section B of the *Agreement* in the instant case constitutes, by implication, a waiver of all preceding grievance processing time limits is not persuasive. First, the obligation referred to is a mutual one, and the evidence (Union Exhibit #1) indicates *joint responsibility/culpability* for the delay. Second, the *Agreement* does not specify any penalty for delays in petitioning the FMCS for a panel of arbitrators.

Finally, any argument that the Employer waived its right to challenge the grievance on arbitrability grounds by not raising this issue prior to the arbitration hearing simply is not supported by the evidence. The Employer first raised timeliness as a bar to arbitration (that is, to further advancement within the grievance framework up to and including arbitration) at Step 3 and at the outset of/prior to the arbitration hearing.

B. ARBITRABILITY

The instant dispute then reduces to one of whether the Step 3 Appeal was hand delivered to a representative of the Employer within the 5 working days after the latter's response at Step 2 as specified by Article 36, Section I, paragraph 2 of the *Agreement*.

Richard Wires, Director of the Cost Analysis and Estimating Division testified that he gave and discussed the Step 2 Response with the Grievant and his Union representative on June 6, 1988. Although Steward William Shockley testified that he attempted to deliver the Step 3 Appeal to a substitute secretary for the Manufacturing Technology Department on June 9, 1988 and that, because she refused to give him a receipted copy of said appeal, he instead delivered it to Labor Relations Specialist Charlotte Shelley, who did provide him with a receipted copy, neither Melissa Hampton, Secretary for the Director of the Manufacturing Technology Department, nor Charlotte Shelley, Labor Relations Specialist, could recall, respectively, the attempt to deliver or the actual delivery of the Step 3 Appeal. Charlotte Shelley was quite emphatic about this fact as the following testimony illustrates:

Q: And you have no recollection that William Shockley delivered this document to you.

A: None whatsoever.

On the contrary, Melissa Hampton testified that the Step 3 Appeal arrived in the AOC mail on June 14, 1988 at 1330 hours and that she so noted this fact on the lower right hand side of the Step 3 Appeal (Management Exhibit #1).

The Arbitrator finds it extremely disconcerting that, at this juncture with the burden of proof having shifted to the Union with the foregoing testimony, it chose not to rebut the latter by providing the receipted copy of the Step 3 Appeal that it allegedly had obtained from Charlotte Shelley. This is precisely the circumstance—that is, a claim of procedural nonarbitrability—for which the receipt was originally sought and presumably retained. It is hard to believe that such a document that the Union fought so doggedly to obtain would not be produced at this time. The Arbitrator can only infer from the Union's failure to produce the disputed document that it does not and did not exist.

In light of the foregoing testimony and evidence, the Arbitrator is compelled to conclude that the weight (i.e., preponderance) of evidence indicates that the time limits for appealing (i.e., advancing) the Step 2 Decision to Step 3 were not met and that, consequently, the instant dispute focusing upon preselection and preferential treatment is not arbitrable.

C. FORFEITURE

A significant number of arbitrators have held that doubts as to the meaning of contractual time limits or as to whether they have been met should be resolved against forfeiture of the right to process the grievance. In this instance, however, there are no such doubts as to either the meaning of the time limits or whether they were met. Under such circumstances as these, the body of arbitral thought is compelling that failure to observe grievance processing time limits will terminate the grievance.*

While the law may abhor forfeitures, arbitral case law absolutely prohibits the disregard of clear contract language, consistent contract applications, and the record of evidence produced during the arbitration hearing—all of which combine to mandate dismissal of the grievance in the instant case. The Arbitrator does not take lightly the forfeiture of this or any other employee's right to process grievances. Yet, the arbitrator is a creature of contract, draws his authority therefrom, and must be found by the clear language thereof in rendering his decision. To do differently would undermine the integrity not only the arbitration process but the overall collective bargaining process as well; the contract would become meaningless as would the process which created it.

D. BAD FAITH PURSUIT OF NONARBITRABLE GRIEVANCE

Article 37, Section F of the *Agreement* requires the Arbitrator, when requested by a party as he has been requested by the Agency in the instant case, to make a finding "as to whether a clearly nongrievable or nonarbitrable grievance has been pursued in bad faith," in which case, "the Arbitrator shall assess all such fees to the party advancing the grievance." Given the particular facts and circumstances of the instant case, the ruling of nonarbitrability automatically implies that the grievance had been pursued in bad faith— that is, at least one representative of the Union knew that the grievance was not timely yet permitted it to be processed. Since this individual was an agent of the Union, it can therefore be concluded that the Union knowingly pursued a nonarbitrable grievance. The Arbitrator, therefore, has no alternative but to assess the arbitrator's and court reporter's fees to the Union—the party that had advanced the nonarbitrable grievance.

Award

Based upon the stipulations of the parties, the evidence, the facts, and the circumstances of this case, the following award is made:

(1) The Grievance of Carl Lohrey is found to be nonarbitrable. The Employer's motion to dismiss the grievance is granted:

GRIEVANCE DISMISSED

(2) The Union is ordered to compensate the Arbitrator and the Court Reporter for their fees and expenses in accordance with the Arbitrator's ruling under Article 37, Section F of the *Agreement*.

---

* See Arbitrators Stouffer in 53 LA 79, 82; Gibson in 51 LA 837, 840; Nathason in 50 LA 1220, 1222; Krinsky in 48 LA 594, 597; Porter in 47 LA 1057, 1059; Tatum in 41 LA 563, 566; Boothe in 47 LA 336, 339; Strong in 46 LA 767, 768; Teple in 46 LA 338, 345; Roberts in 46 LA 59, 61; Small in 45 LA 257, 258; Loucks in 37 LA 588, 590; Livengood in 27 LA 157, 159.

Recommendation

To prevent future problems of procedural arbitrability and thereby facilitate an effectively functioning grievance procedure, the Arbitrator recommends that the parties negotiate a method for validating the timely processing of grievances from one step to the next step of the grievance procedure. The exact method, be it by way of a receipted and dated copy of the appeal or by secured time clock, is left to the imagination of the parties. This recommendation is simply that—a recommendation; it is not a part of the foregoing *Award*.

Muncie, Indiana
October 1, 1989

Clarence R. Deitsch
Arbitrator

Appendix 2

*Code of Professional Responsibility
for Arbitrators
of Labor-Management Disputes*

Foreword

This "Code of Professional Responsibility for Arbitrators of Labor-Management Disputes" supersedes the "Code of Ethics and Procedural Standards for Labor-Management Arbitration," approved in 1951 by a Committee of the American Arbitration Association, by the National Academy of Arbitrators, and by representatives of the Federal Mediation and Conciliation Service.

Revision of the 1951 Code was initiated officially by the same three groups in October, 1972. The Joint Steering Committee named below was designated to draft a proposal.

Reasons for Code revision should be noted briefly. Ethical considerations and procedural standards are sufficiently intertwined to warrant combining the subject matter of Parts I and II of the 1951 Code under the caption of "Professional Responsibility." It has seemed advisable to eliminate admonitions to the parties (Part III of the 1951 Code) except as they appear incidentally in connection with matters primarily involving responsibilities of arbitrators. Substantial growth of third party participation in dispute resolution in the public sector requires consideration. It appears that arbitration of new contract terms may become more significant. Finally, during the interval of more than two decades, new problems have emerged as private sector grievance arbitration has matured and has become more diversified.

JOINT STEERING COMMITTEE

Chairman
William E. Simkin

Representing American Arbitration Association
Frederick H. Bullen
Donald B. Straus

Representing Federal Mediation and Conciliation Service
Lawrence B. Babcock, Jr.
L. Lawrence Schultz

Representing National Academy of Arbitrators
Sylvester Garrett
Ralph T. Seward   *November 30, 1974*

[Note: The Code was adopted in May 1975 and amended (Section 2C.1.c.) in May 1985.]

Table of Contents

Preamble

Background

Voluntary arbitration rests upon the mutual desire of management   1
and labor in each collective bargaining relationship to develop procedures
for dispute settlement which meet their own particular needs and obligations. No two voluntary systems, therefore, are likely to be identical in
practice. Words used to describe arbitrators (Arbitrator, Umpire, Impartial Chairman, Chairman of Arbitration Board, etc.) may suggest typical
approaches but actual differences within any general type of arrangement
may be as great as distinctions often made among the several types.

Some arbitration and related procedures, however, are not the prod-   2
uct of voluntary agreement. These procedures, primarily but not exclusively
applicable in the public sector, sometimes utilize other third party titles
(Fact Finder, Impasse Panel, Board of Inquiry, etc.). These procedures
range all the way from arbitration prescribed by statute to arrangements
substantially indistinguishable from voluntary procedures.

The standards of professional responsibility set forth in this Code   3
are designed to guide the impartial third party serving in these diverse labor-
management relationships.

Scope of Code

This Code is a privately developed set of standards of professional   4
behavior. It applies to voluntary arbitration of labor-management grievance disputes and of disputes concerning new or revised contract terms.
Both "ad hoc" and "permanent" varieties of voluntary arbitration, private
and public sector, are included. To the extent relevant in any specific case,
it also applies to advisory arbitration, impasse resolution panels, arbitration prescribed by statutes, fact-finding, and other special procedures.

The word "arbitrator," as used hereinafter in the Code, is intended   5
to apply to any impartial person, irrespective of specific title, who serves

in a labor-management dispute procedure in which there is conferred authority to decide issues or to make formal recommendations.

6   The Code is not designed to apply to mediation or conciliation, as distinguished from arbitration, nor to other procedures in which the third party is not authorized in advance to make decisions or recommendations. It does not apply to partisan representatives on tripartite boards. It does not apply to commercial arbitration or to other uses of arbitration outside the labor-management dispute area.

Format of Code

7   **Bold Face** type, sometimes including explanatory material, is used to set forth general principles. *Italics* are used for amplification of general principles. Ordinary type is used primarily for illustrative or explanatory comment.

Application of Code

8   Faithful adherence by an arbitrator to this Code is basic to professional responsibility.

9   The National Academy of Arbitrators will expect its members to be governed in their professional conduct by this Code and stands ready, through its Committee on Ethics and Grievances, to advise its members as to the Code's interpretation. The American Arbitration Association and the Federal Mediation and Conciliation Service will apply the Code to the arbitrators on their rosters in cases handled under their respective appointment or referral procedures. Other arbitrators and administrative agencies may, of course, voluntarily adopt the Code and be governed by it.

10   In interpreting the Code and applying it to charges of professional misconduct, under existing or revised procedures of the National Academy of Arbitrators and of the administrative agencies, it should be recognized that while some of its standards express ethical principles basic to the arbitration profession, others rest less on ethics than on considerations of good practice. Experience has shown the difficulty of drawing rigid lines of distinction between ethics and good practice and this Code does not attempt to do so. Rather, it leaves the gravity of alleged misconduct and the extent to which ethical standards have been violated to be assessed in the light of the facts and circumstances of each particular case.

1

Arbitrator's Qualifications and Responsibilities to the Profession

A. General Qualifications

1. Essential personal qualifications of an arbitrator include honesty, integrity, impartiality and general competence in labor relations matters.   11

An arbitrator must demonstrate ability to exercise these personal qualities faithfully and with good judgment, both in procedural matters and in substantive decisions.   12

a. Selection by mutual agreement of the parties or direct designation by an administrative agency are the effective methods of appraisal of this combination of an individual's potential and performance, rather than the fact of placement on a roster of an administrative agency or membership in a professional association of arbitrators.   13

2. An arbitrator must be as ready to rule for one party as for the other on each issue, either in a single case or in a group of cases. Compromise by an arbitrator for the sake of attempting to achieve personal acceptability is unprofessional.   14

B. Qualifications for Special Cases

1. An arbitrator must decline appointment, withdraw, or request technical assistance when he or she decides that a case is beyond his or her competence.   15

16   a. An arbitrator may be qualified generally but not for specialized assignments. Some types of incentive, work standard, job evaluation, welfare program, pension, or insurance cases may require specialized knowledge, experience or competence. Arbitration of contract terms also may require distinctive background and experience.

17   b. Effective appraisal by an administrative agency or by an arbitrator of the need for special qualifications requires that both parties make known the special nature of the case prior to appointment of the arbitrator.

C. Responsibilities to the Profession

18   **1. An arbitrator must uphold the dignity and integrity of the office and endeavor to provide effective service to the parties.**

19   a. To this end, an arbitrator should keep current with principles, practices and developments that are relevant to his or her own field of arbitration practice.

20   **2. An experienced arbitrator should cooperate in the training of new arbitrators.**

21   **3. An arbitrator must not advertise or solicit arbitration assignments.**

22   a. It is a matter of personal preference whether an arbitrator includes "Labor Arbitrator" or similar notation on letterheads, cards, or announcements. *It is inappropriate, however, to include memberships or offices held in professional societies or listings on rosters of administrative agencies.*

23   b. *Information provided for published biographical sketches, as well as that supplied to administrative agencies, must be accurate.* Such information may include membership in professional organizations (including reference to significant offices held), and listings on rosters of administrative agencies.

2

Responsibilities to the Parties

A. Recognition of Diversity in Arbitration Arrangements

**1. An arbitrator should conscientiously endeavor to understand   24
and observe, to the extent consistent with professional responsibility,
the significant principles governing each arbitration system in which
he or she serves.**

   a. Recognition of special features of a particular arbitration ar-   25
   rangement can be essential with respect to procedural matters and
   may influence other aspects of the arbitration process.

**2. Such understanding does not relieve an arbitrator from a cor-   26
ollary responsibility to seek to discern and refuse to lend approval or
consent to any collusive attempt by the parties to use arbitration for
an improper purpose.**

B. Required Disclosures

**1. Before accepting an appointment, an arbitrator must disclose   27
directly or through the administrative agency involved, any current
or past managerial, representational, or consultative relationship with
any company or union involved in a proceeding in which he or she
is being considered for appointment or has been tentatively designated
to serve. Disclosure must also be made of any pertinent pecuniary
interest.**

   a. The duty to disclose includes membership on a Board of   28
   Directors, full-time or part-time service as a representative or advocate, consultation work for a fee, current stock or bond owner-

ship (other than mutual fund shares or appropriate trust arrangements) or any other pertinent form of managerial, financial or immediate family interest in the company or union involved.

29   **2. When an arbitrator is serving concurrently as an advocate for or representative of other companies or unions in labor relations matters, or has done so in recent years, he or she must disclose such activities before accepting appointment as an arbitrator.**

30   **An arbitrator must disclose such activities to an administrative agency if he or she is on that agency's active roster or seeks placement on a roster. Such disclosure then satisfies this requirement for cases handled under that agency's referral.**

31   a. It is not necessary to disclose names of clients or other specific details. It is necessary to indicate the general nature of the labor relations advocacy or representational work involved, whether for companies or unions or both, and a reasonable approximation of the extent of such activity.

32   b. *An arbitrator on an administrative agency's roster has a continuing obligation to notify the agency of any significant changes pertinent to this requirement.*

33   c. When an administrative agency is not involved, an arbitrator must make such disclosure directly unless he or she is certain that both parties to the case are fully aware of such activities.

34   **3. An arbitrator must not permit personal relationships to affect decision-making.**

35   **Prior to acceptance of an appointment, an arbitrator must disclose to the parties or to the administrative agency involved any close personal relationship or other circumstance, in addition to those specifically mentioned earlier in this section, which might reasonably raise a question as to the arbitrator's impartiality.**

36   a. Arbitrators establish personal relationships with many company and union representatives, with fellow arbitrators, and with fellow members of various professional associations. There should be no attempt to be secretive about such friendships or acquaintances but disclosure is not necessary unless some feature of a particular relationship might reasonably appear to impair impartiality.

4. If the circumstances requiring disclosure are not known to the   37
arbitrator prior to acceptance of appointment, disclosure must be made
when such circumstances become known to the arbitrator.

5. The burden of disclosure rests on the arbitrator. After appropri-   38
ate disclosure, the arbitrator may serve if both parties so desire. If the
arbitrator believes or perceives that there is a clear conflict of interest,
he or she should withdraw, irrespective of the expressed desires of the
parties.

C. Privacy of Arbitration

1. All significant aspects of an arbitration proceeding must be   39
treated by the arbitrator as confidential unless this requirement is waived
by both parties or disclosure is required or permitted by law.

a. Attendance at hearings by persons not representing the par-   40
ties or invited by either or both of them should be permitted only
when the parties agree or when an applicable law requires or permits. Occasionally, special circumstances may require that an arbitrator rule on such matters as attendance and degree of participation
of counsel selected by a grievant.

b. *Discussion of a case at any time by an arbitrator with per-*   41
sons not involved directly should be limited to situations where ad-
vance approval or consent of both parties is obtained or where the
identity of the parties and details of the case are sufficiently obscured
to eliminate any realistic probability of identification.

A commonly recognized exception is discussion of a problem   42
in a case with a fellow arbitrator. *Any such discussion does not relieve*
the arbitrator who is acting in the case from sole responsibility for
the decision and the discussion must be considered as confidential.

Discussion of aspects of a case in a classroom without prior   43
specific approval of the parties is not a violation provided the arbitrator is satisfied that there is no breach of essential confidentiality.

c. *It is a violation of professional responsibility for an arbitrator*   44
to make public an award without the consent of the parties.

An arbitrator may ask the parties whether they consent to the   45 *publication of the award either at the hearing or at the time the award is issued.*

46   (1) *If such question is asked at the hearing it should be asked in writing as follows:*

> *"Do you consent to the submission of the award in this matter for publication?*
>
> ( )   ( )
> YES   NO
>
> *If you consent you have the right to notify the arbitrator within 30 days after the date of the award that you revoke your consent."*

It is desirable but not required that the arbitrator remind the parties at the time of the issuance of the award of their right to withdraw their consent to publication.

47   (2) If the question of consent to the publication of the award is raised at the time the award is issued, the arbitrator may state in writing to each party that failure to answer the inquiry within 30 days will be considered an implied consent to publish.

48   d. It is not improper for an arbitrator to donate arbitration files to a library of a college, university or similar institution without prior consent of all the parties involved. When the circumstances permit, there should be deleted from such donations any cases concerning which one or both of the parties have expressed a desire for privacy. As an additional safeguard, an arbitrator may also decide to withhold recent cases or indicate to the donee a time interval before such cases can be made generally available.

49   e. *Applicable laws, regulations, or practices of the parties may permit or even require exceptions to the above noted principles of privacy.*

D. Personal Relationships with the Parties

50   **1. An arbitrator must make every reasonable effort to conform to arrangements required by an administrative agency or mutually desired by the parties regarding communications and personal relationships with the parties.**

a. *Only an "arm's-length" relationship may be acceptable to*   51
the parties in some arbitration arrangements or may be required by
the rules of an administrative agency. The arbitrator should then
have no contact of consequence with representatives of either party
while handling a case without the other party's presence or consent.

b. *In other situations, both parties may want communications*   52
and personal relationships to be less formal. It is then appropriate
for the arbitrator to respond accordingly.

E. Jurisdiction

1. An arbitrator must observe faithfully both the limitations and   53
inclusions of the jurisdiction conferred by an agreement or other submission under which he or she serves.

2. A direct settlement by the parties of some or all issues in a case,   54
at any stage of the proceedings, must be accepted by the arbitrator
as relieving him or her of further jurisdiction over such issues.

F. Mediation by an Arbitrator

1. When the parties wish at the outset to give an arbitrator authori-   55
ty both to mediate and to decide or submit recommendations regarding residual issues, if any, they should so advise the arbitrator prior
to appointment. If the appointment is accepted, the arbitrator must
perform a mediation role consistent with the circumstances of the case.

a. Direct appointments, also, may require a dual role as media-   56
tor and arbitrator of residual issues. This is most likely to occur in
some public sector cases.

2. When a request to mediate is first made after appointment, the   57
arbitrator may either accept or decline a mediation role.

a. *Once arbitration has been invoked, either party normally has*   58
a right to insist that the process be continued to decision.

b. *If one party requests that the arbitrator mediate and the other*   59
party objects, the arbitrator should decline the request.

60   *c. An arbitrator is not precluded from making a suggestion that he or she mediate. To avoid the possibility of improper pressure, the arbitrator should not so suggest unless it can be discerned that both parties are likely to be receptive. In any event, the arbitrator's suggestion should not be pursued unless both parties readily agree.*

G. Reliance by an Arbitrator on Other Arbitration Awards or on Independent Research

61   **1. An arbitrator must assume full personal responsibility for the decision in each case decided.**

62   *a. The extent, if any, to which an arbitrator properly may rely on precedent, on guidance of other awards, or on independent research is dependent primarily on the policies of the parties on these matters, as expressed in the contract, or other agreement, or at the hearing.*

63   b. When the mutual desires of the parties are not known or when the parties express differing opinions or policies, the arbitrator may exercise discretion as to these matters, consistent with acceptance of full personal responsibility for the award.

H. Use of Assistants

64   **1. An arbitrator must not delegate any decision-making function to another person without consent of the parties.**

65   *a. Without prior consent of the parties, an arbitrator may use the services of an assistant for research, clerical duties, or preliminary drafting under the direction of the arbitrator, which does not involve the delegation of any decision-making function.*

66   *b. If an arbitrator is unable, because of time limitations or other reasons, to handle all decision-making aspects of a case, it is not a violation of professional responsibility to suggest to the parties an allocation of responsibility between the arbitrator and an assistant or associate. The arbitrator must not exert pressure on the parties to accept such a suggestion.*

I. Consent Awards

1. Prior to issuance of an award, the parties may jointly request   67
the arbitrator to include in the award certain agreements between them,
concerning some or all of the issues. If the arbitrator believes that a
suggested award is proper, fair, sound, and lawful, it is consistent with
professional responsibility to adopt it.

   a. *Before complying with such a request, an arbitrator must*   68
be certain that he or she understands the suggested settlement ade-
quately in order to be able to appraise its terms. If it appears that
pertinent facts or circumstances may not have been disclosed, the ar-
bitrator should take the initiative to assure that all significant aspects
of the case are fully understood. To this end, the arbitrator may re-
quest additional specific information and may question witnesses at
a hearing.

J. Avoidance of Delay

1. It is a basic professional responsibility of an arbitrator to plan   69
his or her work schedule so that present and future commitments will
be fulfilled in a timely manner.

   a. *When planning is upset for reasons beyond the control of*   70
the arbitrator, he or she, nevertheless, should exert every reasonable
effort to fulfill all commitments. If this is not possible, prompt notice
at the arbitrator's initiative should be given to all parties affected.
Such notices should include reasonably accurate estimates of any
additional time required. To the extent possible, priority should be
given to cases in process so that other parties may make alternative
arbitration arrangements.

2. An arbitrator must cooperate with the parties and with any ad-   71
ministrative agency involved in avoiding delays.

   a. *An arbitrator on the active roster of an administrative agen-*   72
cy must take the initiative in advising the agency of any scheduling
difficulties that he or she can foresee.

   b. *Requests for services, whether received directly or through*   73
an administrative agency, should be declined if the arbitrator is una-
ble to schedule a hearing as soon as the parties wish. If the parties,

nevertheless, jointly desire to obtain the services of the arbitrator and the arbitrator agrees, arrangements should be made by agreement that the arbitrator confidently expects to fulfill.

74   c. *An arbitrator may properly seek to persuade the parties to alter or eliminate arbitration procedures or tactics that cause unnecessary delay.*

75   **3. Once the case record has been closed, an arbitrator must adhere to the time limits for an award, as stipulated in the labor agreement or as provided by regulation of an administrative agency or as otherwise agreed.**

76   a. *If an appropriate award cannot be rendered within the required time, it is incumbent on the arbitrator to seek an extension of time from the parties.*

77   b. If the parties have agreed upon abnormally short time limits for an award after a case is closed, the arbitrator should be so advised by the parties or by the administrative agency involved, prior to acceptance of appointment.

K. Fees and Expenses

78   **1. An arbitrator occupies a position of trust in respect to the parties and the administrative agencies. In charging for services and expenses, the arbitrator must be governed by the same high standards of honor and integrity that apply to all other phases of his or her work.**

79   **An arbitrator must endeavor to keep total charges for services and expenses reasonable and consistent with the nature of the case or cases decided.**

80   **Prior to appointment, the parties should be aware of or be able readily to determine all significant aspects of an arbitrator's bases for charges for fees and expenses.**

a. *Services Not Primarily Chargeable on a Per Diem Basis*

81   By agreement with the parties, the financial aspects of many "permanent" arbitration assignments, of some interest disputes, and of some "ad hoc" grievance assignments do not include a per diem fee for services as a primary part of the total understanding. *In such*

situations, the arbitrator must adhere faithfully to all agreed-upon arrangements governing fees and expenses.

b. *Per Diem Basis for Charges for Services*

(1) *When an arbitrator's charges for services are determined*   82
primarily by a stipulated per diem fee, the arbitrator should establish in advance his or her bases for application of such per diem fee and for determination of reimbursable expenses.

Practices established by an arbitrator should include the basis   83
for charges, if any, for:
(a) hearing time, including the application of the stipulated basic per diem hearing fee to hearing days of varying lengths;
(b) study time;
(c) necessary travel time when not included in charges for hearing time;
(d) postponement or cancellation of hearings by the parties and the circumstances in which such charges will normally be assessed or waived;
(e) office overhead expenses (secretarial, telephone, postage, etc.);
(f) the work of paid assistants or associates.

(2) *Each arbitrator should be guided by the following general*   84
principles:

(a) *Per diem charges for a hearing should not be in excess*   85
of actual time spent or allocated for the hearing.

(b) *Per diem charges for study time should not be in excess*   86
of actual time spent.

(c) *Any fixed ratio of study days to hearing days, not agreed*   87
to specifically by the parties, is inconsistent with the per diem method of charges for services.

(d) *Charges for expenses must not be in excess of actual ex-*   88
penses normally reimbursable and incurred in connection with the case or cases involved.

(e) *When time or expense charges are involved for two or*   89
more sets of parties on the same day or trip, such time or expense charges should be appropriately prorated.

90   (f) *An arbitrator may stipulate in advance a minimum charge for a hearing without violation of (a) or (e) above.*

91   (3) *An arbitrator on the active roster of an administrative agency must file with the agency his or her individual bases for determination of fees and expenses if the agency so requires. Thereafter, it is the responsibility of each such arbitrator to advise the agency promptly of any change in any basis for charges.*

92   Such filing may be in the form of answers to a questionnaire devised by an agency or by any other method adopted by or approved by an agency.

93   *Having supplied an administrative agency with the information noted above, an arbitrator's professional responsibility of disclosure under this Code with respect to fees and expenses has been satisfied for cases referred by that agency.*

94   (4) *If an administrative agency promulgates specific standards with respect to any of these matters which are in addition to or more restrictive than an individual arbitrator's standards, an arbitrator on its active roster must observe the agency standards for cases handled under the auspices of that agency, or decline to serve.*

95   (5) *When an arbitrator is contacted directly by the parties for a case or cases, the arbitrator has a professional responsibility to respond to questions by submitting his or her bases for charges for fees and charges.*

96   (6) *When it is known to the arbitrator that one or both of the parties cannot afford normal charges, it is consistent with professional responsibility to charge lesser amounts to both parties or to one of the parties if the other party is made aware of the difference and agrees.*

97   (7) *If an arbitrator concludes that the total of charges derived from his or her normal basis of calculation is not compatible with the case decided, it is consistent with professional responsibility to charge lesser amounts to both parties.*

98   **2. An arbitrator must maintain adequate records to support charges for services and expenses and must make an accounting to the parties or to an involved administrative agency on request.**

3

Responsibilities to Administrative Agencies

A. General Responsibilities

**1. An arbitrator must be candid, accurate, and fully responsive   99
to an administrative agency concerning his or her qualifications, availability, and all other pertinent matters.**

**2. An arbitrator must observe policies and rules of an administra-   100
tive agency in cases referred by that agency.**

**3. An arbitrator must not seek to influence an administrative agen-   101
cy by any improper means, including gifts or other inducements to
agency personnel.**

   a. It is not improper for a person seeking placement on a roster   102
   to request references from individuals having knowledge of the applicant's experience and qualifications.

   b. Arbitrators should recognize that the primary responsibility of   103
   an administrative agency is to serve the parties.

4

Prehearing Conduct

104   **1. All prehearing matters must be handled in a manner that fosters complete impartiality by the arbitrator.**

105   a. The primary purpose of prehearing discussions involving the arbitrator is to obtain agreement on procedural matters so that the hearing can proceed without unnecessary obstacles. If differences of opinion should arise during such discussions and, particularly, if such differences appear to impinge on substantive matters, the circumstances will suggest whether the matter can be resolved informally or may require a prehearing conference or, more rarely, a formal preliminary hearing. When an administrative agency handles some or all aspects of the arrangements prior to a hearing, the arbitrator will become involved only if differences of some substance arise.

106   b. *Copies of any prehearing correspondence between the arbitrator and either party must be made available to both parties.*

5

Hearing Conduct

A. General Principles

1. An arbitrator must provide a fair and adequate hearing which   107
assures that both parties have sufficient opportunity to present their
respective evidence and argument.

   a. *Within the limits of this responsibility, an arbitrator should*   108
conform to the various types of hearing procedures desired by the
parties.

   b. An arbitrator may: encourage stipulations of fact; restate the   109
substance of issues or arguments to promote or verify understanding; question the parties' representatives or witnesses, when necessary
or advisable, to obtain additional pertinent information; and request
that the parties submit additional evidence, either at the hearing or
by subsequent filing.

   c. *An arbitrator should not intrude into a party's presentation*   110
so as to prevent that party from putting forward its case fairly and
adequately.

B. Transcripts or Recordings

1. Mutual agreement of the parties as to use or non-use of a   111
transcript must be respected by the arbitrator.

   a. *A transcript is the official record of a hearing only when both*   112
parties agree to a transcript or an applicable law or regulation so
provides.

   b. An arbitrator may seek to persuade the parties to avoid use of   113
a transcript, or to use a transcript if the nature of the case appears

to require one. *However, if an arbitrator intends to make his or her appointment to a case contingent on mutual agreement to a transcript, that requirement must be made known to both parties prior to appointment.*

114   c. If the parties do not agree to a transcript, an arbitrator may permit one party to take a transcript at its own cost. The arbitrator may also make appropriate arrangements under which the other party may have access to a copy, if a copy is provided to the arbitrator.

115   d. Without prior approval, an arbitrator may seek to use his or her own tape recorder to supplement note taking. The arbitrator should not insist on such a tape recording if either or both parties object.

C. Ex Parte Hearings

116   **1. In determining whether to conduct an ex parte hearing, an arbitrator must consider relevant legal, contractual, and other pertinent circumstances.**

117   **2. An arbitrator must be certain, before proceeding ex parte, that the party refusing or failing to attend the hearing has been given adequate notice of the time, place, and purposes of the hearing.**

D. Plant Visits

118   **1. An arbitrator should comply with a request of any party that he or she visit a work area pertinent to the dispute prior to, during, or after a hearing. An arbitrator may also initiate such a request.**

119   *a. Procedures for such visits should be agreed to by the parties in consultation with the arbitrator.*

E. Bench Decisions or Expedited Awards

120   **1. When an arbitrator understands, prior to acceptance of appointment, that a bench decision is expected at the conclusion of the hearing, the arbitrator must comply with the understanding unless both parties agree otherwise.**

a. *If notice of the parties' desire for a bench decision is not given   121
prior to the arbitrator's acceptance of the case, issuance of such a
bench decision is discretionary.*

b. *When only one party makes the request and the other ob-   122
jects, the arbitrator should not render a bench decision except under
most unusual circumstances.*

**2. When an arbitrator understands, prior to acceptance of appoint-   123
ment, that a concise written award is expected within a stated time period after the hearing, the arbitrator must comply with the understanding
unless both parties agree otherwise.**

6

Post Hearing Conduct

A. Post Hearing Briefs and Submissions

124   **1. An arbitrator must comply with mutual agreements in respect to the filing or nonfiling of post hearing briefs or submissions.**

125   a. An arbitrator, in his or her discretion, may either suggest the filing of post hearing briefs or other submissions or suggest that none be filed.

126   b. When the parties disagree as to the need for briefs, an arbitrator may permit filing but may determine a reasonable time limitation.

127   **2. An arbitrator must not consider a post hearing brief or submission that has not been provided to the other party.**

B. Disclosure of Terms of Award

128   **1. An arbitrator must not disclose a prospective award to either party prior to its simultaneous issuance to both parties or explore possible alternative awards unilaterally with one party, unless both parties so agree.**

129   a. Partisan members of tripartite boards may know prospective terms of an award in advance of its issuance. Similar situations may exist in other less formal arrangements mutually agreed to by the parties. In any such situation, the arbitrator should determine and observe the mutually desired degree of confidentiality.

C. Awards and Opinions

1. The award should be definite, certain, and as concise as possible.   130

    a. When an opinion is required, factors to be considered by an   131
arbitrator include: desirability of brevity, consistent with the nature
of the case and any expressed desires of the parties; need to use a
style and form that is understandable to responsible representatives
of the parties, to the grievant and supervisors, and to others in the
collective bargaining relationship; necessity of meeting the significant
issues; forthrightness to an extent not harmful to the relationship of
the parties; and avoidance of gratuitous advice or discourse not essential to disposition of the issues.

D. Clarification or Interpretation of Awards

1. No clarification or interpretation of an award is permissible   132
without the consent of both parties.

2. Under agreements which permit or require clarification or inter-   133
pretation of an award, an arbitrator must afford both parties an oppor-
tunity to be heard.

E. Enforcement of Award

1. The arbitrator's responsibility does not extend to the enforce-   134
ment of an award.

2. In view of the professional and confidential nature of the arbitra-   135
tion relationship, an arbitrator should not voluntarily participate in legal
enforcement proceedings.

Appendix 3

*American Arbitration Rules
and Federal Mediation
and Conciliation Regulations*

Voluntary Labor Arbitration Rules

1. Agreement of Parties
The parties shall be deemed to have made these rules a part of their arbitration agreement whenever, in a collective bargaining agreement or submission, they have provided for arbitration by the American Arbitration Association (hereinafter the AAA) or under its rules. These rules and any amendment thereof shall apply in the form obtaining at the time the arbitration is initiated.

2. Name of Tribunal
Any tribunal constituted by the parties under these rules shall be called the Voluntary Labor Arbitration Tribunal.

3. Administrator
When parties agree to arbitrate under these rules and an arbitration is instituted thereunder, they thereby authorize the AAA to administer the arbitration. The authority and obligations of the administrator are as provided in the agreement of the parties and in these rules.

4. Delegation of Duties
The duties of the AAA may be carried out through such representatives or committees as the AAA may direct.

5. Panel of Labor Arbitrators
The AAA shall establish and maintain a Panel of Labor Arbitrators and shall appoint arbitrators therefrom, as hereinafter provided.

6. Office of Tribunal
The general office of the Voluntary Labor Arbitration Tribunal is the headquarters of the AAA, which may, however, assign the administration of an arbitration to any of its regional offices.

7. Initiation under an Arbitration Clause in a Collective Bargaining Agreement
Arbitration under an arbitration clause in a collective bargaining agreement under these rules may be initiated by either party in the following manner:

(a) By giving written notice to the other party of intention to arbitrate (Demand), which notice shall contain a statement setting forth the nature of the dispute and the remedy sought, and

(b) By filing at any regional office of the AAA three copies of said notice, together with a copy of the collective bargaining agreement, or such parts thereof as relate to the dispute, including the arbitration provisions. After the arbitrator is appointed, no new or different claim may be submitted except with the consent of the arbitrator and all other parties.

8. Answer
The party upon whom the Demand for arbitration is made may file an answering statement with the AAA within seven days after notice from the AAA, simultaneously sending a copy to the other party. If no answer is filed within the stated time, it will be assumed that the claim is denied. Failure to file an answer shall not operate to delay the arbitration.

9. Initiation under a Submission
Parties to any collective bargaining agreement may initiate an arbitration under these rules by filing at any regional office of the AAA two copies of a written agreement to arbitrate under these rules (Submission), signed by the parties and setting forth the nature of the dispute and the remedy sought.

10. Fixing of Locale
The parties may mutually agree upon the locale where the arbitration is to be held. If the locale is not designated in the collective bargaining agreement or Submission, and if there is a dispute as to the appropriate locale, the AAA shall have the power to determine the locale and its decision shall be binding.

11. Qualifications of Arbitrator
No person shall serve as a neutral arbitrator in any arbitration in which he or she has any financial personal interest in the result of the arbitration, unless the parties, in writing, waive such disqualification.

12. Appointment from Panel
If the parties have not appointed an arbitrator and have not provided any other method of appointment, the arbitrator shall be appointed in the following manner: Immediately after the filing of the Demand or Submission, the AAA shall submit simultaneously to each party an identical list of names of persons chosen from the Panel of Labor Arbitrators. Each party shall have seven days from the mailing date in which to cross off any names to which it objects, number the remaining names to indicate

the order of preference, and return the list to the AAA. If a party does not return the list within the time specified, all persons named therein shall be deemed acceptable. From among the persons who have been approved on both lists, and in accordance with the designated order of mutual preference, the AAA shall invite the acceptance of an arbitrator to serve. If the parties fail to agree upon any of the persons named, if those named decline or are unable to act, or if for any other reason the appointment cannot be made from the submitted lists, the administrator shall have the power to make the appointment from among other members of the panel without the submission of any additional list.

13. Direct Appointment by Parties

If the agreement of the parties names an arbitrator or specifies a method of appointing an arbitrator, that designation or method shall be followed. The notice of appointment, with the name and address of such arbitrator, shall be filed with the AAA by the appointing party.

If the agreement specifies a period of time within which an arbitrator shall be appointed and any party fails to make such appointment within that period, the AAA may make the appointment.

If no period of time is specified in the agreement, the AAA shall notify the parties to make the appointment and if within seven days thereafter such arbitrator has not been so appointed, the AAA shall make the appointment.

14. Appointment of Neutral Arbitrator by Party-Appointed Arbitrators

If the parties have appointed their arbitrators, or if either or both of them have been appointed as provided in Section 13, and have authorized such arbitrators to appoint a neutral arbitrator within a specified time and no appointment is made within such time or any agreed extension thereof, the AAA may appoint a neutral arbitrator who shall act as chairperson.

If no period of time is specified for appointment of the neutral arbitrator and the parties do not make the appointment within seven days from the date of the appointment of the last party-appointed arbitrator, the AAA shall appoint such neutral arbitrator, who shall act as chairperson.

If the parties have agreed that the arbitrators shall appoint the neutral arbitrator from the panel, the AAA shall furnish to the party-appointed arbitra-

tors, in the manner prescribed in Section 12, a list selected from the panel, and the appointment of the neutral arbitrator shall be made as prescribed in that section.

15. Number of Arbitrators

If the arbitration agreement does not specify the number of arbitrators, the dispute shall be heard and determined by one arbitrator, unless the parties otherwise agree.

16. Notice to Arbitrator of Appointment

Notice of the appointment of the neutral arbitrator shall be mailed to the arbitrator by the AAA and the signed acceptance of the arbitrator shall be filed with the AAA prior to the opening of the first hearing.

17. Disclosure by Arbitrator of Disqualification

Prior to accepting the appointment, the prospective neutral arbitrator shall disclose any circumstance likely to create a presumption of bias or that the arbitrator believes might disqualify him or her as an impartial arbitrator. Upon receipt of such information, the AAA shall immediately disclose it to the parties. If either party declines to waive the presumptive disqualification, the vacancy thus created shall be filled in accordance with the applicable provisions of these rules.

18. Vacancies

If any arbitrator should resign, die, withdraw, refuse, be unable, or be disqualified to perform the duties of office, the AAA shall, on proof satisfactory to it, declare the office vacant. Vacancies shall be filled in the same manner as that governing the making of the original appointment, and the matter shall be reheard by the new arbitrator.

19. Time and Place of Hearing

The arbitrator shall fix the time and place for each hearing. At least five days prior thereto, the AAA shall mail notice of the time and place of hearing to each party, unless the parties otherwise agree.

20. Representation by Counsel

Any party may be represented at the hearing by counsel or by another authorized representative.

21. Stenographic Record

Any party wishing a stenographic record shall make arrangements directly with a stenographer and shall notify the other parties of such arrangements in advance of the hearing. The requesting party or parties shall pay the cost of such record. If such transcript is agreed by the parties to be, or in appropriate cases determined by the arbitrator to be, the official record of the proceeding, it must be made available to the arbitrator and to the other party for inspection, at a time and place determined by the arbitrator.

22. Attendance at Hearings

Persons having a direct interest in the arbitration are entitled to attend hearings. The arbitrator shall have the power to require the retirement of any witness or witnesses during the testimony of other witnesses. It shall be discretionary with the arbitrator to determine the propriety of the attendance of any other person.

23. Adjournments

The arbitrator for good cause shown may adjourn the hearing upon the request of a party or upon his or her own initiative, and shall adjourn when all of the parties agree thereto.

24. Oaths

Before proceeding with the first hearing, each arbitrator may take an oath of office and, if required by law, shall do so. The arbitrator may require witnesses to testify under oath administered by any duly qualified person and, if required by law or requested by either party, shall do so.

25. Majority Decision

Whenever there is more than one arbitrator, all decisions of the arbitrators shall be by majority vote. The award shall also be made by majority vote unless the concurrence of all is expressly required.

26. Order of Proceedings

A hearing shall be opened by the filing of the oath of the arbitrator, where required; by the recording of the place, time, and date of the hearing and the presence of the arbitrator, the parties, and counsel, if any; and by the receipt by the arbitrator of the Demand and answer, if any, or the Submission.

Exhibits may, when offered by either party, be received in evidence by the arbitrator. The names and addresses of all witnesses and exhibits in order received shall be made a part of the record.

The arbitrator may vary the normal procedure under which the initiating party first presents its claim, but in any case shall afford full and equal opportunity to all parties for the presentation of relevant proofs.

27. Arbitration in the Absence of a Party

Unless the law provides to the contrary, the arbitration may proceed in the absence of any party who, after due notice, fails to be present or fails to obtain an adjournment. An award shall not be made solely on the default of a party. The arbitrator shall require the other party to submit such evidence as may be required for the making of an award.

28. Evidence

The parties may offer such evidence as they desire and shall produce such additional evidence as the arbitrator may deem necessary to an understanding and determination of the dispute. An arbitrator authorized by law to subpoena witnesses and documents may do so independently or upon the request of any party. The arbitrator shall be the judge of the relevance and materiality of the evidence offered and conformity to legal rules of evidence shall not be necessary. All evidence shall be taken in the presence of all of the arbitrators and all of the parties except where any of the parties is absent in default or has waived the right to be present.

29. Evidence by Affidavit and Filing of Documents

The arbitrator may receive and consider the evidence of witnesses by affidavit, giving it only such weight as seems proper after consideration of any objection made to its admission.

All documents that are not filed with the arbitrator at the hearing, but arranged at the hearing or subsequently by agreement of the parties to be submitted, shall be filed with the AAA for transmission to the arbitrator. All parties shall be afforded opportunity to examine such documents.

30. Inspection

Whenever the arbitrator deems it necessary, he or she may make an inspection in connection with the subject matter of the dispute after written notice to the parties, who may, if they so desire, be present at such inspection.

31. Closing of Hearings

The arbitrator shall inquire of all parties whether they have any further proofs to offer or witnesses to be heard. Upon receiving negative replies, the arbitrator shall declare the hearings closed and a minute thereof shall be recorded. If briefs or other documents are to be filed, the hearings shall be declared closed as of the final date set by the arbitrator for filing with the AAA. The time limit within which the arbitrator is required to make an award shall commence to run, in the absence of another agreement by the parties, upon the closing of the hearings.

32. Reopening of Hearings

The hearings may for good cause shown be reopened by the arbitrator at will or on the motion of either party at any time before the award is made, but, if the reopening of the hearings would prevent the making of the award within the specific time agreed upon by the parties in the contract out of which the controversy has arisen, the matter may not be reopened unless both parties agree upon the extension of such time. When no specific date is fixed in the contract, the arbitrator may reopen the hearings and shall have thirty days from the closing of the reopened hearings within which to make an award.

33. Waiver of Oral Hearings

The parties may provide, by written agreement, for the waiver of oral hearings. If the parties are unable to agree as to the procedure, the AAA shall specify a fair and equitable procedure.

34. Waiver of Rules

Any party who proceeds with the arbitration after knowledge that any provision or requirement of these rules has not been complied with and who fails to state an objection thereto in writing shall be deemed to have waived the right to object.

35. Extensions of Time

The parties may modify any period of time by mutual agreement. The AAA may for good cause extend any period of time established by these rules, except the time for making the award. The AAA shall notify the parties of any such extension of time and its reason therefor.

36. Serving of Notice

Each party to a Submission or other agreement that provides for arbitration under these rules shall be deemed to have consented and shall consent that any papers, notices, or process necessary or proper for the initiation or continuation of an arbitration under these rules; for any court action in connection therewith; or for the entry of judgment on an award made thereunder may be served upon such party by mail addressed to such party or its attorney at the last known address or by personal service, within or without the state wherein the arbitration is to be held.

37. Time of Award

The award shall be rendered promptly by the arbitrator and, unless otherwise agreed by the parties or specified by law, no later than thirty days from

the date of closing the hearings or, if oral hearings have been waived, from the date of transmitting the final statements and proofs to the arbitrator.

38. Form of Award

The award shall be in writing and shall be signed either by the neutral arbitrator or by a concurring majority if there be more than one arbitrator. The parties shall advise the AAA whenever they do not require the arbitrator to accompany the award with an opinion.

39. Award upon Settlement

If the parties settle their dispute during the course of the arbitration, the arbitrator may, upon their request, set forth the terms of the agreed settlement in an award.

40. Delivery of Award to Parties

Parties shall accept as legal delivery of the award the placing of the award or a true copy thereof in the mail by the AAA, addressed to such party at its last known address or to its attorney; personal service of the award; or the filing of the award in any other manner that may be prescribed by law.

41. Release of Documents for Judicial Proceedings

The AAA shall, upon the written request of a party, furnish to such party, at its expense, certified facsimiles of any papers in the AAA's possession that may be required in judicial proceedings relating to the arbitration.

42. Judicial Proceedings and Exclusion of Liability

(a) Neither the AAA nor any arbitrator in a proceeding under these rules is a necessary party in judicial proceedings relating to the arbitration.

(b) Neither the AAA nor any arbitrator shall be liable to any party for any act or omission in connection with any arbitration conducted under these rules.

43. Administrative Fees

As a not-for-profit organization, the AAA shall prescribe an administrative fee schedule to compensate it for the cost of providing administrative services. The schedule in effect at the time of filing shall be applicable.

44. Expenses

The expenses of witnesses for either side shall be paid by the party producing such witnesses.

Expenses of the arbitration, other than the cost of

the stenographic record, including required travel-
ing and other expenses of the arbitrator and of
AAA representatives and the expenses of any
witness or the cost of any proof produced at the
direct request of the arbitrator, shall be borne
equally by the parties, unless they agree otherwise,
or unless the arbitrator, in the award, assesses
such expenses or any part thereof against any
specified party or parties.

45. Communication with Arbitrator

There shall be no communication between the
parties and a neutral arbitrator other than at oral
hearings. Any other oral or written communication
from the parties to the arbitrator shall be directed
to the AAA for transmittal to the arbitrator.

46. Interpretation and Application of Rules

The arbitrator shall interpret and apply these rules
insofar as they relate to the arbitrator's powers and
duties. When there is more than one arbitrator
and a difference arises among them concerning the
meaning or application of any such rule, it shall
be decided by a majority vote. If that is unobtain-
able, the arbitrator or either party may refer the
question to the AAA for final decision. All other
rules shall be interpreted and applied by the AAA.

Federal Mediation and Conciliation Service

Subpart A: Arbitration Policy; Administration of Roster

1404.1 Scope and Authority

This chapter is issued by the Federal Mediation and Conciliation Service (FMCS) under Title II of
the Labor Management Relations Act of 1947 (Public
Law 80-101) as amended in 1959 (Public Law 86-257)
and 1974 (Public Law 93-360). The chapter applies to
all arbitrators listed on the FMCS Roster of Arbitrators,
to all applicants for listing on the Roster, and to all persons or parties seeking to obtain from FMCS either
names or panels of names of arbitrators listed on the
Roster in connection with disputes which are to be
submitted to arbitration or fact-finding.

1404.2 Policy

The labor policy of the United States is designed to promote the settlement of issues between
employers and represented employees through the
processes of collective bargaining and voluntary arbitration. This policy encourages the use of voluntary
arbitration to resolve disputes over the interpretation or
application of collective bargaining agreements. Voluntary arbitration and fact-finding in disputes and disagreements over establishment or modification of contract
terms are important features of constructive labor-
management relations, as alternatives to economic
strife in the settlement of labor disputes.

1404.3 Administrative Responsibilities

(a) *Director.* The Director of FMCS has ultimate responsibility for all aspects of FMCS arbitration
activities and is the final agency authority on all questions concerning the Roster or FMCS arbitration procedures.

(b) *Office of Arbitration Services.* The Office
of Arbitration Services (OAS) maintains a Roster of
Arbitrators (the "Roster"); administers Subpart C of
these Regulations (Procedures for Arbitration Services); assists, promotes, and cooperates in the establishment of programs for training and developing new
arbitrators; collects information and statistics concerning the arbitration function, and performs other tasks in
connection with the function that may be assigned by
the Director.

(c) *Arbitrator Review Board.* The Arbitrator
Review Board (the "Board") shall consist of a presiding
officer and such members and alternate members as
the Director may appoint, and who shall serve at the
Director's pleasure and may be removed at any time.
The Board shall be composed entirely of full-time offi-
cers or employees of the Federal Government. The
Board shall establish its own procedures for carrying
out its duties.

(1) *Duties of the Board.* The Board shall:

(i) Review the qualifications of all applicants
for listing on the Roster, interpreting and
applying the criteria set forth in subsection
1404.5 of this part;

(ii) Review the status of all persons whose
continued eligibility for listing on the Roster
has been questioned under subsection 1404.5
of this part;

(iii) Make recommendations to the Director
regarding acceptance or rejection of applicants for listing on the Roster, or regarding
withdrawal of listing on the Roster for any of
the reasons set forth herein.

Subpart B: Roster of Arbitrators; Admission and Retention

1404.4 Roster and Status of Members

(a) *The Roster.* The FMCS shall maintain a Roster of labor arbitrators consisting of persons who meet the criteria for listing contained in subsection 1404.5 of this part and whose names have not been removed from the Roster in accordance with subsection 1404.5(d).

(b) *Adherence to Standards and Requirements.* Persons listed on the Roster shall comply with the FMCS rules and regulations pertaining to arbitration and with such guidelines and procedures as may be issued by OAS pursuant to Subpart C hereof. Arbitrators are also expected to conform to the ethical standards and procedures set forth in the Code of Professional Responsibility for Arbitrators of Labor Management Disputes, as approved by the Joint Steering Committee of the National Academy of Arbitrators.

(c) *Status of Arbitrators.* Persons who are listed on the Roster and are selected or appointed to hear arbitration matters or to serve as factfinders do not become employees of the Federal Government by virtue of their selection or appointment. Following selection or appointment, the arbitrator's relationship is solely with the parties to the dispute, except that arbitrators are subject to certain reporting requirements and to standards of conduct as set forth in this Part.

(d) *Role of FMCS.* FMCS has no power to:

(1) Compel parties to arbitrate or agree to arbitration;
(2) Enforce an agreement to arbitrate;
(3) Compel parties to agree to a particular arbitrator;
(4) Influence, alter or set aside decisions of arbitrators listed on the Roster;
(5) Compel, deny or modify payment of compensation to an arbitrator.

(e) *Nominations and Panels.* On request of the parties to an agreement to arbitrate or engage in fact-finding, or where arbitration or fact-finding may be provided for by statute, OAS will provide names or panels of names without charge. Procedures for obtaining these services are contained in Subpart C. Neither the submission of a nomination or panel nor the appointment of an arbitrator constitutes a determination by FMCS that an agreement to arbitrate or enter fact-finding proceedings exists; nor does such action constitute a ruling that the matter in controversy is arbitrable under any agreement.

(f) *Rights of Persons Listed on the Roster.* No person shall have any right to be listed or to remain listed on the Roster. FMCS retains the authority and responsibility to assure that the needs of the parties using its facilities are served. To accomplish this purpose it may establish procedures for the preparation of panels or the appointment of arbitrators or factfinders which include consideration of such factors as background and experience, availability, acceptability, geographical location and the expressed preferences of the parties.

1404.5 Listing on the Roster; Criteria for Listing and Retention

Persons seeking to be listed on the Roster must complete and submit an application form which may be obtained from the Office of Arbitration Services. Upon receipt of an executed form, OAS will review the application, assure that it is complete, make such inquiries as are necessary, and submit the application to the Arbitrator Review Board. The Board will review the completed applications under the criteria set forth in subsections (a), (b) and (c) of this Section, and will forward to the Director its recommendation on each applicant. The Director makes all final decisions as to whether an applicant may be listed. Each applicant shall be notified in writing of the Director's decision and the reasons therefore.

(a) *General Criteria.* Applicants for the Roster will be listed on the Roster upon a determination that they:

(1) Are experienced, competent and acceptable in decision-making roles in the resolution of labor relations disputes; or
(2) Have extensive experience in relevant positions in collective bargaining; and
(3) Are capable of conducting an orderly hearing, can analyze testimony and exhibits and can prepare clear and concise findings and awards within reasonable time limits.

(b) *Proof of Qualifications.* The qualifications listed in (a) above are preferably demonstrated by the submission of actual arbitration awards prepared by the applicant while serving as an impartial arbitrator chosen by the parties to disputes. Equivalent experience acquired in training, internship or other development programs, or experience such as that acquired as a hearing officer or judge in labor relations controversies may also be considered by the Board.

(c) *Advocacy.*

(1) Definition. An advocate is a person who represents employers, labor organizations, or individuals as an employee, attorney or consultant, in matters of labor relations, including but not limited to the subjects of union representation and recognition matters, collective bargaining, arbitration, unfair labor practices, equal employment opportunity and other areas generally recognized as constituting labor relations. The definition includes representatives of employers or employees in individual cases or controversies involving workmen's compensation, occupational health or safety, minimum wage or other labor standards matters.

The definition of advocate also includes a person who is directly associated with an advocate in a business or professional relationship as, for example, partners or employees of a law firm.

(2) Eligibility. Except in the case of persons listed on the Roster before November 17, 1976, no person who is an advocate, as defined above, may be listed. No person who was listed on the Roster at any time who was not an advocate when listed or who did not divulge advocacy at the time of listing may continue to be listed after becoming an advocate or after the fact of advocacy is revealed.

(d) *Duration of Listing, Retention.* Initial listing may be for a period not to exceed three years, and may be renewed thereafter for periods not to exceed two years, provided upon review that this listing is not cancelled by the Director as set forth below. Notice of cancellation may be given to the member whenever the member;

(1) No longer meets the criteria for admission;

(2) Has been repeatedly and flagrantly delinquent in submitting awards;

(3) Has refused to make reasonable and periodic reports to FMCS, as required in Subpart C, concerning activities pertaining to arbitration;

(4) Has been the subject of complaints by parties who use FMCS facilities, and the Director, after appropriate inquiry, concludes that just cause for cancellation has been shown;

(5) Is determined by the Director to be unacceptable to the parties who use FMCS arbitration facilities; the Director may base a determination of unacceptability on FMCS records showing the number

of times the arbitrator's name has been proposed to the parties and the number of times it has been selected.

No listing may be cancelled without at least sixty days notice of the reasons for the proposed removal, unless the Director determines that the FMCS or the parties will be harmed by continued listing. In such cases an arbitrator's listing may be suspended without notice or delay pending final determination in accordance with these procedures. The member shall in either case have an opportunity to submit a written response showing why the listing should not be cancelled. The Director may, at his discretion, appoint a hearing officer to conduct an inquiry into the facts of any proposed cancellation and to make recommendations to the Director.

1404.6 Freedom of Choice

Nothing contained herein should be construed to limit the rights of parties who use FMCS arbitration facilities to select jointly any arbitrator or arbitration procedure acceptable to them.

Subpart C: Procedures for Arbitration Services

1404.10 Procedures for Requesting Arbitration Panels

The Office of Arbitration Services has been delegated the responsibility for administering all requests for arbitration services under these regulations.

(a) The Service will refer a panel of arbitrators to the parties upon request. The Service prefers to act upon a joint request which should be addressed to the Federal Mediation and Conciliation Service, Washington, D.C. 20427, Attention: Office of Arbitration Services. In the event that the request is made by only one party, the Service will submit a panel; however, any submission of a panel should not be construed as anything more than compliance with a request and does not necessarily reflect the contractual requirements of the parties.

(b) The parties are urged to use the Request for Arbitration Panel form (R-43) which has been prepared by the Service and is available in quantity at all FMCS regional offices and field stations or upon request to the Federal Mediation and Conciliation Service, Office of Arbitration Services, Washington, D.C. 20427. The form R-43 is reproduced herein for the purpose of identification.

(c) A brief statement of the issues in dispute should accompany the request and enable the Service to submit the names of arbitrators qualified for the issues involved. The request should also include a current copy of the arbitration section of the collective bargaining agreement or stipulation to arbitrate.

(d) If form R-43 is not utilized, the parties may request a panel by letter which must include the names, addresses, and phone numbers of the parties, the location of the contemplated hearing, the issue in dispute, the number of names desired on the panel, the industry involved and any special qualifications of the panel or special requirement desired.

1404.11 Arbitrability

Where either party claims that a dispute is not subject to arbitration, the Service will not decide the merits of such claim.

FMCS Form R-43
Sep 1975

FEDERAL MEDIATION AND CONCILIATION SERVICE
WASHINGTON, D.C. 20437

Form Approved
OMB No. 21-R0007

REQUEST FOR ARBITRATION PANEL

To: Director, Arbitration Services
Federal Mediation and Conciliation Service
Washington, D.C. 20427

Copy No. 1, Original - To Federal Mediation and Conciliation Service

1404.12 Nominations of Arbitrators

(a) When the parties have been unable to agree on an arbitrator, the Service will submit to the parties on request the names of seven arbitrators unless the applicable collective bargaining agreement provides for a different number, or unless the parties themselves request a different number. Together with the submission of a panel of arbitrators, the Service will furnish a biographical sketch for each member of the panel. This sketch states the background, qualifications, experience, and per diem fee established by the arbitrator. It states the existence, if any, of other fees such as cancellation, postponement, rescheduling or administrative fees.

(b) When a panel is submitted, an FMCS control case number is assigned. All future communications between the parties and the Service should refer to the case number.

(c) The Service considers many factors when selecting names for inclusion on a panel, but the agreed-upon wishes of the parties are paramount. Special qualifications of arbitrators experienced in certain issues or industries, or possessing certain backgrounds, may be identified for purposes of submitting panels to accommodate the parties. The Service may also consider such things as general acceptability, geographical location, general experience, availability, size of fee, and the need to expose new arbitrators to the selection process in preparing panels. The Service has no obligation to put an individual on any given panel, or on a minimum number of panels in any fixed period, such as a month or a year.

(1) If at any time both parties request, for valid reasons, that a name or names be omitted from a panel, such name or names will be omitted, unless they are excessive in number.

(2) If at any time both parties request that a name or names be included on a panel, such name or names will be included.

(3) If only one party requests that a name or names be omitted from a panel, or that specific individuals be added to the panel, such request shall not be honored.

(4) If the issue described in the request appears to require special technical experience or qualifications, arbitrators who possess such qualifications will, where possible, be included on the panel submitted to the parties.

(5) In almost all cases, an arbitrator is chosen from one panel. However, if either party requests another panel, the Service shall comply with the request providing that an additional panel is permissible under the terms of the agreement or the other party so agrees. Requests for more than two panels must be accompanied by a statement of explanation

and will be considered on a case-by-case basis.

1404.13 Selection and Appointment of Arbitrators

(a) The parties should notify the OAS of their selection of an arbitrator. The arbitrator, upon notification by the parties, shall notify the OAS of his selection and willingness to serve. Upon notification of the parties' selection of an arbitrator, the Service will make a formal appointment of the arbitrator.

(b) Where the contract is silent on the manner of selecting arbitrators, the parties may wish to consider one of the following methods for selection of an arbitrator from a panel:

(1) Each party alternately strikes a name from the submitted panel until one remains.
(2) Each party advises the Service of its order of preference by numbering each name on the panel and submitting the numbered list in writing to OAS. The name on the panel that has the lowest accumulated numerical number will be appointed.
(3) Informal agreement of the parties by whatever method they choose.
(c) The Service will, on joint or unilateral request of the parties, submit a panel or, when the applicable collective bargaining agreement authorizes, will make a direct appointment of an arbitrator. Submission of a panel or name signifies nothing more than compliance with a request and in no way constitutes a determination by the Service that the parties are obligated to arbitrate the dispute in question. Resolution of disputes as to the propriety of such a submission or appointment rests solely with the parties.

(d) The arbitrator, upon notification of appointment, is required to communicate with the parties immediately to arrange for preliminary matters, such as date and place of hearing.

1404.14 Conduct of Hearings

(a) All proceedings conducted by the arbitrator shall be in conformity with the contractual obligations of the parties. The arbitrator is also expected to conduct all proceedings in conformity with Section 1404.4(b). The conduct of the arbitration proceeding is under the arbitrator's jurisdiction and control and the arbitrator's decision is to be based upon the evidence and testimony presented at the hearing or otherwise incorporated in the record of the proceeding. The arbitrator may, unless prohibited by law, proceed in the absence of any party who, after due notice, fails to be

present or to obtain a postponement. An award rendered in an *ex parte* proceeding of this nature must be based upon evidence presented to the arbitrator.

1404.15 Decision and Award

(a) Arbitrators are encouraged to render awards not later than 60 days from the date of the closing of the record as determined by the arbitrator, unless otherwise agreed upon by the parties or specified by law. A failure to render timely awards reflects upon the performance of an arbitrator and may lead to his removal from the FMCS Roster.

(b) The parties should inform the OAS whenever a decision is unduly delayed. The arbitrator shall notify the OAS if and when the arbitrator (1) cannot schedule, hear and determine issues promptly, or; (2) learns a dispute has been settled by the parties prior to the decision.
(c) After an award has been submitted to the parties, the arbitrator is required to submit a Fee and Award Statement, form R-19 showing a breakdown of the fee and expense charges so that the Service may be in a position to review conformance with stated charges under Section 1404.12(a). Filing the Statement within 15 days after rendering an award is required of all arbitrators. The Statements are not used for the purpose of compelling payment of fees.

(d) The Service encourages the publication of arbitration awards. However, the Service expects arbitrators it has nominated or appointed not to give publicity to awards they issue if objected to by one of the parties.

1404.16. Fees and Charges of Arbitrators

(a) No administrative or filing fee is charged by the Service. The current policy of the Service permits each of its nominees or appointees to charge a per diem fee and other predetermined fees for services, the amount of which has been certified in advance to the Service. Each arbitrator's maximum per diem fee and the existence of other predetermined fees, if any, are set forth on a biographical sketch which is sent to the parties when panels are submitted and are the controlling fees. The arbitrator shall not change any fee or add charges without giving at least 30 days advance notice to the Service.

(b) In cases involving unusual amounts of time and expenses relative to pre-hearing and post-hearing administration of a particular case, an administrative charge may be made by the arbitrator.

(c) All charges other than those specified by 1404.16(a) shall be divulged to and agreement obtained by the arbitrator with the parties immediately after appointment.

(d) The Service requests that it be notified of any arbitrator's deviation from the policies expressed herein. However, the Service will not attempt to resolve any fee dispute.

1404.17 Reports and Biographical Sketches

(a) Arbitrators listed on the Roster shall execute and return all documents, forms and reports required by the Service. They shall also keep the Service informed of changes of address, telephone number, availability, and of any business of other connection or relationship which involves labor-management relations, or which creates or gives the appearance of advocacy as defined in Section 1404.4(c)(1).

(b) The Service may require each arbitrator listed on the Roster to prepare at the time of initial listing, and to revise, biographical information in accordance with a format to be provided by the Service at the time of initial listing or biennial review. Arbitrators may also request revision of biographical information at other times to reflect changes in fees, the existence of additional charges, address, experience or background, or other relevant data. The Service reserves the right to decide and approve the format and content of biographical sketches.

Rights Arbitration: Contract Interpretation

ARBITRATION OPINION AND AWARD

(IN RE WALNUT GROVE EDUCATION ASSOCIATION)
(AND)
(WALNUT GROVE SCHOOL CORPORATION)
(AAA CASE NO. 00 000 0000 00 E)
(GRIEVANCE: TEACHER TRANSFER DENIED)

ARBITRATOR:

DR. CLARENCE R. DEITSCH
MUNCIE, INDIANA
SELECTED BY THE PARTIES
THROUGH THE PROCEDURES
OF THE AMERICAN ARBITRATION
ASSOCIATION

DATE OF GRIEVANCE: April 27, 1989
DATE OF HEARING: September 21, 1989
DATE OF AWARD: November 18, 1989

Appearances: For the Union: Robert Abrell, UniServe Director, Indiana Classroom Teachers Association. For the Employer: Paul J. Baxter, Attorney.

TEACHER TRANSFER DENIAL

The Issue

DEITSCH, Arbitrator—Whether the School Corporation violated Article 8(C)(1)(d) of the *Agreement* when it failed to grant the Grievant's request for a voluntary transfer. If so, what should the remedy be?

Stipulated Evidence

1. All procedural requirements specified by the *Agreement* for the arbitration of the instant grievance were met; the issue/matter is properly before the Arbitrator.

2. Both applicants for the open position (i.e., transfer) were certified.

3. The School Corporation's decision was not based on a "formal evaluation of prior performance."

4. Both applicants have six (6) years of service under regular contract with the School Corporation. Since both signed their first contracts on the same day—August 25, 1981, relative seniority was determined by examining birthdates as specified by the *Agreement*. The Grievant is the more senior of the two applicants because her birthdate precedes that of the other applicant.

5. The decisional criteria listed in Article 8(C)(1)(d) are not arranged in rank order of importance; all are to be weighted equally.

6. Joint Exhibit #1A: *Agreement* between the Walnut Grove Education Association and the Walnut Grove School Corporation, 1977–79, specifically those articles pertaining to reduction in force and transfers.

7. Joint Exhibit #1B: 1979–81 *Agreement*, specifically those articles pertaining to reduction in force and transfers.

8. Joint Exhibit #1C: 1981–84 *Agreement*, specifically those articles pertaining to reduction in force and transfers.

9. Joint Exhibit #1D: 1984–85 *Agreement*, specifically those articles pertaining to reduction in force and transfers.

10. Joint Exhibit #1E: *Agreement* between the Walnut Grove Education Association and the Walnut Grove School Corporation, 1986–89—the instant contract.

11. Joint Exhibit #2: The Grievant's Request for Transfer, dated 4/19/89.

12. Joint Exhibit #3: Principal Chris Bousman's Memorandum to Ralph W. Cavanaugh, Assistant Superintendent of Personnel, dated 4/22/89, justifying/explaining his selection of Mrs. Shirley A. Cole for the open first grade position instead of the Grievant, Joyce M. Dalton.

13. Joint Exhibit #4: The Grievance of Joyce M. Dalton, dated 4/27/89.

14. Joint Exhibit #5: Mr. Chris Bousman's Response to the Grievance, dated 5/2/89.

15. Joint Exhibit #6: The Professional Staff Performance Evaluations of the Grievant, Joyce M. Dalton.

16. Joint Exhibit #7: The Professional Staff Performance Evaluations of the Successful Position Applicant, Shirley A. Cole.

17. Joint Exhibit #8: The Job Posting for the First Grade Position at C. O. Harrison School, dated 4/14/88.

18. Joint Exhibit #9: Ralph W. Cavanaugh's Letter to Robert Abrell detailing the experience of Shirley A. Cole and the Grievant, dated 9/15/89.

Relevant Contract Provisions

Article 1: Recognition

B. Definitions
   8. The term "Seniority" shall mean any certified person's period of employment under a regular teacher's contract in the Walnut Grove School Corporation (not necessarily continuous), including approved leaves of absence and layoffs. Seniority begins to accumulate on the date the Corporation approves a regular teacher's contract for that person. When two or more teachers have the same seniority, the teacher that signed his individual contract with the school corporation on the earliest date shall be considered most senior. If two or more teachers signed their individual contracts on the same date, then the teacher with the earliest birthdate shall be considered senior.

Article 2: Management Rights

A. The School Corporation reserves all the rights enumerated in the General School Powers Act of 1965 as amended.
B. Specifically, the School Corporation shall have the responsibility and authority to manage and direct in behalf of the public the operations and activities of this school corporation to the full extent authorized by law. Such responsibility and activity shall include but not be limited to the right of the school employer to:
   1. Direct the work of its employees;
   2. Establish policy;
   3. Hire, promote, demote, transfer, assign and retain employees;
   4. Suspend or discharge its employees in accordance with applicable law;
   5. Maintain the efficiency of school operations;
   6. Relieve its employees from duties because of lack of work or other legitimate reasons;
   7. Take whatever actions are necessary to carry out the mission of the public schools as provided by law.

Article 7: Reduction in Force

If or when it becomes necessary for the School Corporation to reduce the certified staff due to economic necessity or declining enrollment, the following provisions will apply:

A. In General

    .

    .

    .

6. Elementary teachers' classification is K–6. Secondary classification (7–12) is by subject area.

B. Reduction Within a Building

1. When a reduction of the number of teachers in a school is necessary, a volunteer shall, whenever possible, be granted a transfer first.

2. In the absence of volunteers, the teacher with the shortest length of service in the system who is teaching in the classification which is being reduced shall be involuntarily displaced.

3. A teacher who is to be involuntarily transferred shall be notified by the Assistant Superintendent–Instruction prior to receiving written notice of such transfer. Consideration shall be given to the time necessary for preparation of room and materials.

4. When involuntary transfers are necessary, a list of vacancies in existence at that time in other schools shall be made available to all teachers being transferred. In filling such vacancies, preferences shall be given to presently employed teachers over newly hired teachers.

5. If there are no vacancies in existence, the displaced teacher shall have the right to bump the teacher with the least seniority in the classification for which the displaced teacher is certified; however, if a displaced teacher is not certified for a position held by a less senior teacher, the School Corporation shall not be required to assign him portions of other teachers' assignments, nor shall it be required to reassign another teacher in order to create a position for which the displaced teacher is certified.

C. System-Wide Reductions

1. For Permanent Teachers, systemwide reductions shall be based on the following criteria:

    (a) Certification

    (b) Seniority

    Affected Permanent Teachers shall receive a list reflecting vacancies in other schools as well as potential openings which will become available as a result of the bumping process. Selections will be made from this list in order of seniority.

Article 8: Reassignment, Transfer and Vacancies

A. The terms reassignment and transfer are defined as follows:

1. Reassignment is a change of a teacher assignment within the school where

presently assigned, which at the secondary level means a change in subject area and at the elementary level means a change in grade level.

2. Transfer is change of assignment from one building to another.

B. The procedures for effecting reassignment within a school are as follows:
   1. Voluntary Reassignment
      a. As they become known, all vacancies which occur within a given elementary building shall be posted in that building for no less than three (3) working days.
      b. Any teacher currently assigned to the building in which the vacancy occurs who desires a change in grade and/or subject assignment shall file a Form A with the building principal.
      c. Selection shall be based on the following criteria:
         1. Greatest length of service in the system.
         2. Proper certification for the classification.
         3. Prior experience in the classification, which at the secondary level means subject area and at the elementary level means grade level.

C. Transfers
   1. Voluntary
      a. Teachers who desire to transfer to another building shall submit Form B (see Appendix D) to the Assistant Superintendent–Instruction.
      b. Transfer requests for posted vacancies must be received in the office of the Assistant Superintendent–Instruction during the posting period.
      c. The Assistant Superintendent–Instruction shall acknowledge in writing, within five (5) working days, the receipt of the request.
      d. The criteria to be used in making the decision shall be as follows:
         1. Greatest length of service in the system.
         2. Certification.
         3. Prior experience in the classification.
         4. Formal evaluation of prior performance.
   2. Involuntary
      a. In the absence of volunteers, the teacher with the shortest length of service in the system who is teaching in the classification which is being reduced in a given school shall be involuntarily displaced.
      b. A teacher who is affected by an involuntary transfer shall be notified by the Assistant Superintendent–Instruction prior to receiving written notice of such change. Consideration shall be given to the time necessary for preparation of room and materials.
      c. When involuntary transfers are necessary, a list of vacancies in existence at that time in other schools shall be made available to all teachers being transferred. In filling such vacancies, preference shall be given to presently employed teachers over newly hired teachers.
      d. If there are no vacancies in existence, the displaced teacher shall have the right to bump the teacher with the least seniority in a classification for which the displaced teacher is certified; however, if a displaced teacher is not certified for a position held by a less senior teacher, the School

Corporation shall not be required to assign him portions of other teachers' assignments, nor shall it be required to reassign another teacher in order to create a position for which the displaced teacher is certified.

Background

On 4/14/89, a first grade teaching position at C. O. Harrison School was posted as available for the 1989–90 school year (Joint Exhibit #8). The Grievant, Joyce M. Dalton, requested a transfer to that opening on 4/19/89 (Joint Exhibit #2). She was interviewed for that position by the Principal of C. O. Harrison School, Chris Bousman, on 4/21/89 (Joint Exhibit #5). On 4/22/89, Principal Bousman sent a memo to Assistant Superintendent Cavanaugh requesting that Mrs. Shirley A. Cole be granted the transfer to the open position instead of the Grievant. Reasons cited for the selection included "Mrs. Cole's varied teaching experiences" and "Junior Great Books training" (Joint Exhibit #3). The Grievant was notified on 4/26/89 that her transfer request had been denied. Principal Bousman's transfer decision was grieved by Mrs. Joyce M. Dalton on 4/27/89 (Joint Exhibit #4). On 5/2/89, Principal Bousman sent a letter to the Grievant explaining the reasons for not honoring her transfer request.

Positions of the Parties

The following positions were taken by the Walnut Grove Education Association and the Walnut Grove School Corporation, respectively, in a hearing before the Arbitrator on Wednesday, September 20, 1989 at the Administration Building, 909 East Main Street, Walnut Grove, Indiana and by post hearing briefs received on Wednesday, October 25, 1989.

Union:

Article 8(C)(1)(d) of the *Agreement* establishes four (4) specific criteria to be used in deciding which of a number of applicants requesting a transfer shall be granted said transfer, namely:

1. Greatest length of service in the system.
2. Certification.
3. Prior experience in the classification.
4. Formal evaluation of prior performance.

All criteria carry equal weight in the determination of the successful applicant for transfer.

Both Mrs. Shirley A. Cole and the Grievant are equally qualified for transfer on the basis of the "certification criterion." With respect to each of the three remaining criteria, however, the Grievant is more deserving of (qualified for) transfer; she should have received the transfer per these contractually established criteria.

With regard to "greatest length of service in the system," the Grievant had the advantage—regardless of whether this criterion is interpreted to mean seniority or length of time employed in the District. If interpreted to mean seniority, the Grievant is most senior. She has the same number of regular contract years of service, the same original contract signing date, *but* an earlier birthdate. According to Article 1(B)8 of the *Agree-*

ment, therefore, she is the most senior and should have been selected for transfer. If interpreted to mean length of time employed in the District, the Grievant again has the advantage because she has six and one-half (6 1/2) years of service to the District [six (6) years under regular contract and one-half year under temporary contract] while Mrs. Shirley A. Cole only has six (6) years of service to the District (all under regular contract—Union Exhibit #'s 2 and 3). In short, the Grievant has the advantage on the criterion of "greatest length of service in the system" no matter how that is to be interpreted.

The same holds true for the "formal evaluation of prior performance" criterion. Although the formal evaluations of each applicant's prior performance are similar in that both are good, the Grievant's are clearly better. Specifically, the Grievant received excellent ratings on specified performance items twenty-two percent (22%) of the time while Mrs. Cole received excellent ratings on these same performance items only eleven percent (11%) of the time (Joint Exhibit #'s 6 and 7). Once again the Grievant meets the criterion better than the party granted the transfer.

The final and most disputed criterion is "prior experience in the classification." The Association maintains that this means "length of service" in "grade level" and not, as the District maintains, "variety of experiences" in "K–6." That the Association's interpretation of classification is the correct one is immediately obvious from a comparison of 1981–84 contract language with 1984–85 contract language. The earlier contract contained the definition of classification as used by the District namely, "K–6," in Article 6, *REDUCTION IN FORCE* (RIF). Although this definition was retained in subsequent contracts for RIF purposes, the parties saw a need to add new language—a new definition—for reassignments, transfers, vacancies, and summer assignments. Accordingly, the 1984–85 contract defined classification to mean "grade level" in Article 7(B)1(a)3, *REASSIGNMENT, TRANSFER, VACANCIES, AND SUMMER SCHOOL ASSIGNMENTS*. Hence, it is this definition of classification (i.e., "grade level") and not the former (i.e., "K–6") that governs reassignments and transfers.

The Association's interpretation of experience as "length of service" rather than "types and kinds of *experiences*" is also correct. The use of the singular "experience" rather than the plural "experiences," the commonly understood meaning of the word "experience" in the education profession, the definition of the word "experience" found in *Black's Law Dictionary*, and bargaining history all speak to the correctness of the Association's interpretation of experience as "length of service" as opposed to "types and kinds of experiences."

The final criterion, therefore, for purposes of determining transfers is "length of service in grade level" = "prior experience in the classification." Here, as in the case of the other criteria, the Grievant has the advantage. She has four years of experience at the first grade level while Mrs. Shirley A. Cole only has one year of experience (Joint Exhibit #9).

In summary, three of the four criteria specified in the *Agreement* mandate selection of the Grievant for transfer. Except for certification where they were equal, the Grievant was more qualified on each criterion than was Mrs. Cole. It is for this reason that the Association requests the Arbitrator to uphold the grievance and order the District to comply with the *Agreement* and offer the transfer to the Grievant.

Employer:

Article 8(C)(1)(d) of the *Agreement* establishes four (4) criteria for purposes of determining which of a number of applicants for a voluntary transfer shall be granted the transfer, namely:

1. Greatest length of service in the system.
2. Certification.
3. Prior experience in the classification.
4. Formal evaluation of prior performance.

The parties stipulated that each criterion carries equal weight in the determination of the successful applicant for transfer and that both Mrs. Shirley A. Cole and the Grievant were equally qualified with regard to the "certification criterion." The District's position is that, since neither candidate had an advantage with regard to the "greatest length of service in the system" and "formal evaluation of prior performance" criteria, the decision was based on the "prior experience in the classification" criterion. Here, the clear advantage/edge belonged to Mrs. Cole and not the Grievant—because of Cole's prior experience and training in the "Big Books Reading Program." The District's transfer decision, therefore, did not violate the terms of the *Agreement*.

The Association contends that "length of service in the system" is synonymous with "seniority" defined in Article 1(B)8 and that, consequently, the Grievant, because of her earlier birthdate (the second tiebreaker for purposes of determining seniority where length of service is the same), is more senior than Mrs. Cole, thus having a clear edge with respect to this criterion. The Association's position is clearly incorrect. When the term "seniority" was introduced in the 1981–1984 *Agreement*, the parties' clear intention was to restrict its application to system-wide reductions in force involving permanent and semi-permanent teachers [Article 7(C)(1)–(2) of the current *Agreement*] and to determining the "bumping" rights of involuntarily transferred teachers where vacancies do not exist [Article 8(C)(2)(d) of the current *Agreement*]. It was never intended to be applied to reductions in force involving nonpermanent teachers [Article 7(C)(3) of the current *Agreement*] or to the article entitled "Reassignment, Transfer and Vacancies" [Article 8 of the current *Agreement*]—with the exception of the bumping procedure noted above. Instead, the language "length of service in the system" was retained and was to be applied to these matters.

The Association's only expert witness testified to this intent—acknowledged that seniority as defined in Article 1(B)(8) is applicable only to reduction in force and involuntary transfers leading to reductions in force, and not to reassignments or transfers unassociated with a layoff. This witness, Mark D. Kendall, was uniquely qualified to testify as to the intent of the parties because he was a former president of the Walnut Grove Education Association, a past spokesperson for the negotiating team, and had served on those teams that had negotiated the disputed language. The evidence is clear, therefore, that "length of service in the system" is not synonymous with seniority.

Nor can the Association take the position that "length of service in the system" includes service to the system under temporary contract, thereby giving the edge to the Grievant on this criterion. To do so would create the totally unacceptable possibility of a teacher with less seniority having more transfer rights than a teacher with greater seniority. Simply put, both the Grievant and Mrs. Cole were equally qualified on the "length of service in the system" criterion; both had six years of service.

The most disputed of the criteria is "prior experience in the classification." The Association contends that "classification" assumes the definition contained in Article 8(B)(1)(c)(3), namely, that it means "grade level." That the correct interpretation of "classification" is "K–6" stems from the need to apply and interpret all provisions of the *Agreement* in a consistent fashion. "K–6" is the clear meaning of "classification" as used in Article 8(C)2 dealing with *involuntary* transfers. Association witness, Mark D. Kendall, agreed with this interpretation. Therefore, by implication, association, and logical consistency, "K–6" is the meaning to be given to "classification" in Article 8(C)1 dealing with *voluntary* transfers—the provisions applicable to the instant dispute. Further, Dr. Harold Allen, Assistant Superintendent for Personnel from 1975 until 1986, Ralph W. Cavanaugh, Assistant Superintendent for Personnel from 1986 until the present, and Chris Bousman, Principal of C. O. Harrison School, were unanimous in their testimony that "classification" had been historically interpreted to mean "K–6" for purposes of transfers—Article 8(C)1–2. "Classification" means "grade level" *only* when the *Agreement* addresses reassignment within a school—Article 8(B). Accordingly, the Grievant did not have an inherent advantage in terms of years of experience—four years of experience at the first grade level/classification (the transfer position) to Mrs. Cole's one year of experience. Instead, both had six years of experience within the classification—"K–6."

With regard to this same criterion, the Association would limit "prior experience" to mean "length of service," thereby precluding the District from considering the types, kinds, and varieties of experience an applicant had had for purposes of determining transfers. Such an interpretation is clearly incorrect. Had the parties intended such, they would have used the phrase "length of service" as they had done two criteria earlier and not "prior experience." The District's expert witnesses—Allen, Cavanaugh, and Bousman—testified that "prior experience" had always been interpreted to include the *nature* as well as the length of the experience within the classification. Since both applicants had the same number of years of experience within the "K–6" classification (i.e., six) and Mrs. Cole had prior experience and training with the "Big Books Reading Program"—the unique type of experience called for by the open position, the clear advantage/edge belonged to Mrs. Cole with regard to the "prior experience in the classification" criterion. Mrs. Cole was more qualified for transfer on the basis of this criterion than the Grievant was.

With regard to the last criterion—"formal evaluation of prior performance," the parties stipulated that the selection was not made on the basis of "formal evaluation of prior performance." Both applicants had good evaluations—for all intents and purposes, identical evaluations. Neither applicant, therefore, possessed an advantage with regard to this criterion.

In summary, the Grievant and Mrs. Cole were equally worthy of transfer on the basis of each of the criteria—except one: "prior experience in the classification." Here, because of her prior experience and training in the "Big Books Reading Program," the clear advantage belonged to Mrs. Cole. Accordingly, she was selected for transfer over the Grievant—in accordance with language and intent of the *Agreement*. The District, therefore, respectfully prays the grievance be denied.

Discussion and Opinion

Since the Association is challenging the propriety of the Corporation's action in this contract interpretation case, it bears the burden of proving a contractual violation. It will be presumed that the Corporation's action denying the Grievant's transfer request was in conformity with the *Agreement* until the Association established by a "preponderance of the evidence" the contrary.

The parties stipulated that both applicants for transfer—the Grievant and Mrs. Cole—

were equally qualified on the basis of the "certification" criterion specified in Article 8(C)(1)(d). They further stipulated that each criterion specified in Article 8(C)(1)(d), namely:

1. Greatest length of service in the system.
2. Certification.
3. Prior experience in the classification.
4. Formal evaluation of prior performance.

was to be given equal weight for purposes of determining transfers. The instant dispute, therefore, reduces to one of which candidate warranted transfer on the basis of the three remaining criteria. Each of these criteria and the merits of each candidate relative thereto are addressed below.

I. GREATEST LENGTH OF SERVICE IN THE SYSTEM

The evidence is incontrovertible that "seniority" and "greatest length of service in the system" are not synonymous. The parties' clear intention was to restrict the totally objective "seniority" criterion to those sections of the *Agreement* addressing the *layoff* of permanent and semi-permanent teachers—namely, Article 7(C)(1)–(2) and Article 8(C)(2)(d)—and to retain "greatest length of service in the system" for those sections of the *Agreement* addressing the layoff of nonpermanent teachers and reassignments, transfers, and vacancies—namely, Article 7(C)3 and Article 8 exclusive of Section 8(C)(2)(d) which deals with bumping-induced layoffs. The Association's only expert witness testified to this intent. This witness, Mark D. Kendall, was well qualified to address the question of intent because he was present throughout the negotiations that produced the disputed language—as a member of the Association's bargaining team.

A cardinal rule of contract construction is that disputed contract language not be interpreted in a fashion that destroys rights or privileges clearly established elsewhere in the labor agreement. The Association's definition of "length of service" as including service in the system under temporary contracts would do just that. Seniority is a valued employee benefit. As an employee acquires seniority, he/she also acquires greater rights under the contract with regard to promotions, job security, better working conditions, and the like. Including service under temporary contracts in computing "greatest length of service in the system" for purposes of preferential selection of teachers for transfer could conceivably create situations where less senior teachers have greater transfer rights than more senior teachers because of greater length of service under temporary contracts— situations totally at odds with the basic concept of seniority embodied in the instant *Agreement*. The definition of "length of service" that would produce such an intolerable state of affairs—the Association's definition, therefore, cannot be accepted by this Arbitrator.

In light of the foregoing arguments, the only acceptable definition of "greatest length of service in the system" is "greatest length of service in the system under regular contract." By this standard, both applicants for transfer were equally qualified; both applicants had six years of service.

II. PRIOR EXPERIENCE IN THE CLASSIFICATION

The Association's position is that "classification" assumes the definition of classification contained in the reassignment section of the Article entitled "Reassignment, Transfer and Vacancies," namely, "grade level," and that "experience" means "length of service." Accordingly, since the Grievant had four years of service at the first grade level (the transfer position) and Mrs. Cole only one (Joint Exhibit #9), the Grievant had a clear advantage/edge with regard to this criterion and should have been granted the transfer. The Corporation, on the other hand, maintains that the Association's definition of classification, namely, "grade level," applies only to teacher reassignment within the school and that the definition of classification applicable to the transfer provisions is "K–6." Accordingly, since both applicants had the same number of years of service—six (Joint Exhibit #9), they were equally qualified for transfer on the basis of this criterion—provided "prior experience" means years of service. The Corporation, however, maintains that "prior experience" transcends length of service and encompasses the nature (i.e., the kind, type, and variety) of the experience as well. It is with regard to the nature of the experience, according to the Corporation, that Mrs. Cole had a clear advantage over the Grievant; she had prior experience and training in the reading program to be implemented in the transfer position.

The Corporation's position is more persuasive on both counts—the meaning of classification and the meaning of prior experience. With regard to classification, the Corporation's three expert witnesses all testified to the fact that classification had always been interpreted as "K–6" for transfer purposes. The Association's own expert witness, Mark D. Kendall, reluctantly agreed to this interpretation of classification for involuntary transfers.

The *parol rules of evidence*—that principle of contract construction that requires the contract to be viewed as a whole and the meaning of disputed provisions determined therefrom—points to the same conclusion—that classification means "K–6." Article 8(c) deals with transfers—voluntary and involuntary alike. It does not contain a definition of classification *per se*. However, the language addressing involuntary transfers is identical to the language of Article 7(B) addressing reductions in force (RIF) within a building. Classification is defined for RIF purposes by Article 7(A) to mean "K–6." Classification must, therefore, be interpreted the same way with regard to involuntary transfers in Article 8(C)—as all four witnesses at the hearing so testified. Hence, logic and consistency—the *parol rules of evidence*—demand the same definition for classification with respect to voluntary transfers (the subject of instant dispute) addressed by that very same Article 8(C).

Webster's New World Dictionary defines "experience" as:

> 1. The act of living through an event 2. anything or everything observed or lived through 3. a) training and personal participation b) knowledge, skill, etc. resulting from this.

This definition clearly contemplates more than simple time served; it encompasses the nature of the experience—the "knowledge, skill, etc. resulting from . . ." what was "observed or lived through." Different kinds of experience produce different skills and, hence, different qualifications. If the parties had intended "prior experience" to be limited to "length of service," they would have used that phrase. After all, it had been used just two lines earlier in establishing the first criterion for transfer. Finally, the Corporation's three expert witnesses all testified that they had always understood/interpreted "prior experience" to mean kinds as well as length of experience.

In short, the clear weight of evidence compels the Arbitrator to conclude that "prior experience in the classification" means "the nature as well as the length of experience

K–6." The Arbitrator further concludes that Mrs. Cole was the more qualified applicant on the basis of this criterion because she had the same number of years of experience K–6 but more experience (i.e., "knowledge, skill, etc.") specific/relevant to the requirements of the transfer position—she had prior experience and training in the "Big Books Reading Program."

III. FORMAL EVALUATION OF PRIOR PERFORMANCE

The parties stipulated that the selection was not made on the basis of "formal evaluation of prior performance." The Association argues that this criterion should have been considered and, if it had been, the Grievant would have had an edge. The Corporation, on the other hand, contends that said argument is improper at this time since this point was not raised at any step of the grievance procedure. Hence, according to the Corporation, it should not be considered by the Arbitrator. The Arbitrator is inclined to agree with the Corporation and will accord it minimal weight.

Of the evaluations of prior performance of both applicants *entered* as Joint Exhibit #'s 6 and 7, there are only two years in which both applicants were evaluated by the same evaluator—1983–84 and 1985–86 when both Mrs. Cole and the Grievant were evaluated by Loretta S. Sherwood. In all other cases, either the applicants were evaluated by different individuals or one of the applicant's evaluations was missing. Where evaluations are as close as they are in the instant case when done by different individuals, minor differences are meaningless because the evaluators may adhere to slightly different standards of excellence. Comparisons thereunder are only slightly better than "comparing apples and oranges." Accordingly, the Arbitrator will only consider the two sets of evaluations done by Mrs. Sherwood for 1983–84 and 1985–86.

Both applicants' evaluations are good. Mrs. Cole's evaluation is *slightly* better than the Grievant's for 1983–84 (four "excellent checks" versus two) while the Grievant's evaluation is slightly better than Mrs. Cole's for 1985–86 (ten "excellent checks" versus seven). For both periods, the Grievant holds an *almost indistinguishable* edge of twelve "excellent checks" to eleven "excellent checks." When the latter is further tempered for the reasons noted above, the applicants are, for all practical purposes, dead even with respect to this last criterion.

IV. MANAGEMENT RIGHTS

Assuming, arguendo, that the Grievant had an advantage with regard to the "formal evaluation of prior performance" criterion, and *given* that Mrs. Cole had an advantage with respect to the "prior experience in the classification" criterion, both candidates would have been equally qualified for transfer under the criteria specified in Article 8(C)(1)(d). Even under this condition—equal qualifications, the Corporation's selection of Mrs. Cole would have been proper and in accord with the *Agreement*. Article 2, Management Rights, reserves to the Corporation the right to "hire, promote, demote, transfer, assign and retain employees" as long as the exercise of these rights does not destroy employee rights enumerated elsewhere in the *Agreement*. The Corporation's selection of Mrs. Cole would not have violated the Article 8(C)(1)(d) rights of the Grievant; both candidates *would* have been equally qualified—the Grievant having no contractual right to preferential transfer. The decision, however, was not this close. Mrs. Cole had an overall advantage on the basis of the "prior experience in the classification" criterion and equal qualifications with respect to the remaining criteria—the Corporation made the correct selection.

In short, the Walnut Grove Education Association *did not establish* by a preponderance of the evidence that the Walnut Grove School Corporation violated Article 8(C)(1)(d) of the *Agreement* when it failed to grant the Grievant's request for a voluntary transfer.

Award

Based upon the stipulations of the parties, the evidence, the facts, and the circumstances of this case, the following award is made:

(1) The Grievance of Joyce M. Dalton is found to be *without* merit. The Corporation's motion to dismiss the Grievance is granted:

GRIEVANCE DENIED

(2) The parties are hereby directed to compensate the Arbitrator for his fee and expenses in accordance with the applicable provision(s) of the *Agreement*.

Muncie, Indiana
November 18, 1989

Clarence R. Deitsch
Arbitrator

Rights Arbitration: Discipline

ARBITRATION OPINION AND AWARD

(IN RE FORT WAYNE COMMUNITY SCHOOLS)
(AND)
(AMERICAN FEDERATION OF STATE, COUNTY)
(AND MUNICIPAL EMPLOYEES, LOCAL 561)

ARBITRATOR:

DR. CLARENCE R. DEITSCH
MUNCIE, INDIANA
SELECTED BY THE PARTIES
THROUGH THE PROCEDURES
OF THE INDIANA DIVISION
OF LABOR

DATE OF HEARING: January 20, 1982
DATE OF AWARD: March 15, 1982

Appearances: For the Employer—William L. Sweet, Jr., attorney. For the Union—Charles S. Brown, attorney.

UNSATISFACTORY PERFORMANCE

The Issue

DEITSCH, Arbitrator: Is the matter arbitrable given the definition of a grievance and the employer's rights specified in the *Policy Booklet for Food Service Employees for 1982*? If the matter is arbitrable, was the Grievant, M, discharged for proper cause? If not, what should the remedy be?

Stipulated Evidence

1. All procedural requirements specified by the *Policy Booklet* for the arbitration of this matter were waived by mutual agreement of the parties to expedite resolution of this dispute through advisory arbitration—including the threshold issue of arbitrability.

2. Joint Exhibit #1: *The Policy Booklet for Food Service Employees for 1981* that served in lieu of a dyed-in-the-wool, formal collective bargaining agreement. Although fashioned bilaterally in discussions between the School Board and the Union, the document was adopted by unilateral School Board action. Both the School Board and the union, however, consider the provisions of the *Policy Booklet* to have the status and force of contractual provisions.

3. Joint Exhibit #2: The Official Grievance Form containing M's written complaint, namely:

I am protesting my discharge at Snider High School. I feel I have been discriminated against by Management. I filed a grievance on October 21, 1981, and since then I have been evaluated two times in November.

The assistant manager has lied against me to the upper management and this is the reason I was fired unjustly. I have been under Doctor care and a letter was turned in specifying light duty work. I have the Seniority for any light job.
—dated December 7, 1981.

4. Joint Exhibit #3: The Work Rules for Classified Employees of Fort Wayne Community Schools, revised 2/19/81.

Background

The Grievant, M, was first employed by Fort Wayne Community Schools on September 27, 1976, as a Cafeteria Assistant. In April 1981, the Grievant's primary responsibilities as a Cafeteria Assistant consisted of setting up the malt machine and operating the cash register. Her annual job evaluation of April 13, 1981, indicates that the Grievant discharged the forenamed job responsibilities in a satisfactory manner.

As a result of remodeling work done in the school cafeteria and in anticipation of increased student traffic, work assignments within the job classification of Cafeteria Assistant were changed for the 1981–82 School Year. Employees were notified of these changes prior to commencement of work in the autumn of 1981. The Grievant's new responsibilities were operating the cash register and assisting in the washing of pots and pans. On October 20, 1981, the Grievant was reassigned from cashier to a la carte server. Several weeks later her job was again changed—this time to a server on the Type A lunch line. On November 3, 1981—after reassignment to the a la carte line but before her transfer to the Type A lunch line—the Grievant received an unsatisfactory job evaluation from her superior, Laura Robinson. She received another unsatisfactory evaluation on November 30, 1981, and was discharged the same day. The Grievant filed her formal complaint on December 7, 1981.

Position of the Parties

The following positions were taken by the Employer and the Union, respectively, in a hearing before the Arbitrator on Wednesday, January 20, 1982, in the Administrative

Center of Fort Wayne Community Schools, and by post hearing briefs submitted to the Arbitrator on or before March 10, 1982.

Employer:

I.

Issue: *Is this matter arbitrable given the definition of a grievance and the employer's rights in the applicable School Board Policies?*

School Board's Position: *A grievance is narrowly defined in the applicable School Board policy as involving only an alleged violation of the policy booklet; this grievance does not involve or allege such a violation, and therefore is not properly presented to arbitration.*

Although there was no formal collective bargaining agreement in effect between the School Board of the Fort Wayne Community Schools and Local 561, the School Board did unilaterally adopt a policy which had been agreed upon in discussions between Board representatives and Local 561. That policy was introduced in evidence as Joint Exhibit 1. Two provisions of that policy are directly applicable here, the section dealing with school employer rights found on page 2 of the policy, and the grievance procedure found on pages 4 and 5 of the policy. Insofar as is relevant here, those sections state as follows:

The school employer has the right, responsibility, and authority to manage and direct on behalf of the public the operations and activities of the school corporation *to the full extent authorized by law.* It is understood and agreed that all rights, responsibility, and authority heretofore exercised by the school employer or inherent in the school employer, the body charged by the law with the operation of the school corporation are retained solely by the school employer. Such rights, responsibilities, and authority of the school employer shall include, but are not limited to, the right to: ... (4) *suspend or discharge its employees in accord with applicable law.* (Emphasis added)

GRIEVANCE PROCEDURE

GENERAL—A grievance shall be defined as a difference between the administration and an employee *involving an alleged violation, misinterpretation, or misapplication of the policies, rules, or regulations contained in this employee policy booklet* ... either the union or the administration may request advisory arbitration. (Emphasis added)

The grievance in this case was introduced into evidence as Joint Exhibit 2. On its face, the grievant protests her discharge. However, the grievance does not allege any violation, misinterpretation, or misapplications of the policies, rules, or regulations contained in the employee policy booklet. Moreover, no such violations were alleged at the arbitration hearing. The reason for that is obvious—there is nothing in the policy booklet protecting an employee's job by prohibiting terminations except for just cause, by requiring progressive discipline, or placing any other restriction on the right of the employer to discharge employees. The fact that the school policy contains no such restrictions, and the fact that a grievance is defined to involve only violations of that policy was done purposefully when the school policy booklet was drafted. By uncontradicted testimony,

Dr. Robert Eastman, the Director of Employee Relations for the schools for some fifteen years, testified that the definitions were intentional and were drawn up so that employee rights were either gained in negotiations and put into the policy booklet, or did not exist. Of course, limiting the definition of a grievance to a violation of a labor contract is not unusual. Most private sector labor contracts define a grievance similarly. However, most of these contracts also require that an employee may not be discharged for just cause, and state therein certain forms of progressive discipline to be followed before a discharge can take place. Those employee rights, however, were won at the bargaining table. What the grievant seeks in this particular case are rights which neither she nor her representative have bargained for.

The only conceivable argument the grievant could make that a violation of the policy booklet occurred is that there is some "applicable law" within the meaning of subparagraph 4 of the employer rights clause. In order to resolve that question, we must look at what laws apply to non-certified school employees.

Certain public employees in this state have job protection by statute. For example, certified employees (teachers) of school systems are protected by what used to be known as the tenure laws. Today, they are classified as either permanent, semi-permanent, or non-permanent employees according to length of service. They do have, however, job protection in the sense that they may only be dismissed for certain specified grounds as explicitly described by statute. Similarly, policemen and firemen may be removed by a Board of Safety of the Municipality only for certain grounds. There are no statutes, however, protecting the rights of non-certified employees of school systems. In the absence of such statutory protection, those employees have rights, if at all, only by contract.

Several Indiana cases have clearly held that in the absence of an explicit employment contract, an employee has no right to continued employment and may be terminated for cause or without any cause at all, *Martin vs. Platt* (1979) 386 N.E. 2d 1026, *Campbell vs. Eli Lilly & Co.* (1980), 413 N.E. 2d 1054. It is thus the law in this state that an employee without a contract, and not protected by statute such as those applicable to teachers, is an employee at will and may be discharged at any time.

That same principle has been recognized by the United States Supreme Court. In a series of cases beginning with *Board of Regents vs. Roth*, 408 U.S. 564, and continuing through *Bishop vs. Wood*, 426 U.S. 341, the Supreme Court recognized that an employee may be discharged at will without even the right to a hearing absent a "property interest." Such a property interest can arise by virtue of tenure laws or by contractual rights prohibiting a discharge except for just cause. The tenure situation was discussed in *Board of Regents vs. Roth*, supra, in which the Court held that an untenured college teacher was not even entitled to any hearing prior to discharge absent a reason for discharge which so impugned his reputation that it would make it difficult, if not impossible, to obtain another job. Thus, it is clear as a matter of law that absent a "just cause" provision in the applicable policy or employment contract, or a state law in the nature of a tenure statute, there is no "applicable law" prohibiting the discharge of this employee, and therefore nothing in the school policy which could be violated or could support a grievance. The only time an employee such as the Food Service worker involved here would even be entitled to a hearing would be if the reasons for the discharge were so serious that they would prevent her from getting another job. She would then be entitled to a hearing of the type established in the School Board's due process procedure, which was introduced into evidence as Board Exhibit 3.

In short, this particular grievant has no employment rights guaranteed to her by Board policy, none by state law, and therefore nothing within the definition of a grievance. This matter is therefore not properly before the arbitrator, and should be dismissed.

II.

Issue: If this grievance is arbitrable, was the grievant discharged for proper cause, and if not, what should the remedy be?

School Board's Position: The grievant was properly discharged for failure to perform the duties of her job after being warned in an evaluation and not improving her performance.

In order to understand the merits of this particular grievance, the arbitrator should review the evidence presented. At the beginning of the school year in the fall of 1981, new jobs were assigned in the high school cafeteria as a result of certain physical changes in the cafeteria and the need to accommodate a substantial number of new students. The grievant was not pleased with her job assignment, and in the early weeks of the school year, had a number of difficulties getting along with students. As a result of those difficulties, her job was changed on October 20 from cashier to a server on the a la carte line. She had problems keeping the line stocked, which was part of her duty, and spent time standing around rather than performing her job. After problems on the a la carte line, several weeks later her job was changed to a server on the Type A lunch line. She again had problems seeing to it that proper portions were delivered to the students, uncovering foods so that students could see the selections, and keeping the line stocked. Generally, her work effort was far below that expected of the rest of the employees, who were quite busy, and her work effort had been substantially diminished since the beginning of the year. She was evaluated on November 3, 1981, as unsatisfactory. After that evaluation, she failed to improve, and she received a second unsatisfactory evaluation on November 30, and was discharged.

These facts were testified to by her supervisor, Laura Robinson, who all witnesses agreed was fair and treated the grievant fairly. They were also verified by the Assistant Principal, the cashier on the other food line, and the a la carte cook.

In response to that evidence, the grievant presented two witnesses who said she did her job in the dish room. Both admitted, however, that the dish room was a small portion of her job. The grievant also claimed that the assistant cafeteria manager had lied about her, and her representative claimed in the arbitration proceeding that her difficulties in getting along were also caused by the assistant manager. However, the grievant's own witnesses testified that the assistant manager had problems with all employees, and there is no evidence whatever that the grievant was singled out for disparate treatment. Moreover, her own witness, Anita Evans, testified that some of the difficulties with the assistant manager were caused by the grievant failing to follow an instruction not to hassle students when there was some confusion over who was entitled to free lunches.

Another claim was raised by the grievant that for some reason the two job evaluations given her in November were strange, and evidence in and of themselves of harassment. However, in Board Exhibit 3, the evaluation policy is clearly stated. An evaluation can take place at any time, and when unsatisfactory, shall be followed by another evaluation not less than two weeks following the first evaluation. In other words, the evaluations done on her were completely consistent with standard Board policy governing all classified employees.

The only evidence presented contrary to the School Board's witnesses was submitted by the grievant herself. She testified that she was instructed by the cafeteria manager to close down her line early and that that was the reason why her line would often have no students, while the other line would have a number still going through. Of course, that does not rebut the testimony that students generally complained about and avoided her line, and it is also inconsistent with her denial that her actions towards students drove them to the other line. She cannot, on the one hand, claim that she had to turn students away and shut down early at the instructions of her supervisor, and on the other, claim that she was only properly charging them for lunches and that that was the reason for diminished student interest in her line. Either the students didn't go because her line shut down, or the students didn't go because she was charging them or they didn't like her. She cannot have it both ways, and her testimony on this point is simply not credible.

The grievant also testified that she could observe the a la carte line, all the way on the other side of the cafeteria, apparently beyond a wall, and could tell that it ran out of food prior to the time she became a server on that line. The grievant's testimony on this point is not credible, either, because if she were doing her job, she would simply not have time to observe a serving line all the way across the cafeteria.

In short, the grievant's attitude toward her job is best summed up by a statement she made during the arbitration hearing and by review of the grievance form itself. At the hearing, she admitted she was mad because "*my* register was taken away from *me*." In her grievance, she claims that she had the seniority for a light job. The fact of the matter is that the grievant did not want to work. She wanted light work, and she wanted to run a cash register. When she didn't get her way, she didn't do her job. She was warned in the first evaluation (Board Exhibit 1). That evaluation was just about as negative as an evaluation can be. When she failed to improve, she was given the second evaluation and terminated. That is what she should have expected.

> Respectfully submitted,
>
> BARRETT, BARRETT & McNAGNY
> William L. Sweet, Jr.
> 395 Lincoln Bank Tower
> P. O. Box 2263
> Fort Wayne, Indiana 46801
> Telephone: (219) 423-9551
>
> Attorneys for Fort Wayne Community
> Schools

Union:

Issue No. 1

The Employer raises the issue of arbitrability and questions whether or not the Employee has the right under the Policy Booklet to grieve her discharge.

The Employer would rely on Joint Exhibit #1, page two thereof, which reserves to the Employer rights to suspend and discharge its employees in accordance with applicable law. The Employer would also infer that there is no provision in the grievance procedure which would grant to the Employee the right to grieve her dismissal.

The Employee submits that under the Recognition Section on page one of the Policy Booklet, Local #561 is given the right to assist employees who "wish to be represented by it concerning grievances, personnel policies and practices, wages, and hours or other matters affecting general working conditions of the designated working employees."

Section IV of the Policy Booklet sets forth the grievance procedure and defines the grievance as a "difference between the administration and an employee involving an alleged violation, misinterpretation or misapplication of the policies, rules, or regulations contained in this employee policy booklet."

It is inconceivable that this grievance is not arbitrable, for to hold otherwise would make a nullity of the grievance procedure set forth in Section IV of the Booklet, and would also make a nullity of the recognition granted to Local #561. The Employer further states that the work rules (Joint Exhibit #3) prohibit the arbitrability of this grievance. The Employer would have us believe that her dismissal did not fall under said rules. In looking at Joint Exhibit #3, we find the statement in paragraph two thereof that the list is not intended to include all types of activity which would lead to discipline, but which is intended to be suggestive of those types of things that would result in disciplinary action. The mere fact that the reason for dismissal herein is not specifically listed, cannot be grounds to defeat the arbitration herein. The rules themselves indicate that not all grounds for discipline are listed. In looking at Elkouri "How Arbitration Works," we find the following at page 611 thereof:

> However, many arbitrators would imply a just cause limitation in any collective agreement. For instance, Arbitrator Walter E. Boles held that "a 'just cause' basis for consideration of disciplinary action is, absent a clear proviso to the contrary, implied in a modern collective bargaining agreement." The reasoning is: "If the Company can discharge without cause, it can lay off without cause. It can recall, transfer, or promote in violation of the seniority provisions simply by invoking its claimed right to discharge. Thus, to interpret the Agreement in accord with claim of the Company would reduce to a nullity the fundamental provision of a labor-management agreement—the security of a worker in his job. Moreover, in at least one case it has been held that management does not have an unrestricted right to discharge at its own discretion even where no bargaining relationship exists, since "the fair and generally accepted understanding of employer-employee relations is that there are obligations on the part of both parties" and that an "obligation on the employer is that an employee shall not be dismissed without cause."

The writer firmly believes that this grievance is arbitrable, for any determination otherwise would remove any right that Local #561, or any employee, from using the grievance procedure set forth in the Policy Booklet.

Issue No. 2

Was there just cause for the dismissal, and if not, what is the appropriate remedy?

Evidence Presented

The Employer presented the evidence of Dr. Eastman to the effect that he had personally handled this discharge himself. That prior to the discharge, the Personnel Department had processed all discharges. On cross-examination, Dr. Eastman had forgotten that, since this discharge, the Personnel Department had reverted to the old system and had terminated a Robert Walker. Dr. Eastman also testified that he had very carefully and deliberately used language in the Policy Booklet in order to limit employee grievances. He further testified that the purpose of the Policy Booklet was to let the employees know their rights and that other employees had been given progressive discipline prior to their termination. That no progressive discipline had been given to the grievant herein.

Laura Robinson, Supervisor, testified that the grievant had had good evaluations during the five years of employment, and in fact on April 13, 1981, had received a good evaluation. She further testified that an incident arose in October concerning free lunches, which was thereafter resolved as not being the fault of the grievant. Her testimony indicated that her Assistant Manager may have created the difficulty in October, 1981, and that her Assistant Manager had had problems in the past with getting along with other employees. She further testified that she did not consider the October incident in reaching her decision in terminating the grievant.

The Assistant Principal testified that the grievant had a poor relationship with the students, challenged students in the lunch line, sometimes rightfully challenging said students. The Assistant Principal had had no discussions with the grievant and to her knowledge the first problem was the October, 1981 incident concerning the free lunch.

Witnesses presented by the grievant indicated she kept busy, was a good worker, always willing and very helpful to other employees. Co-worker Woodward further testified that the Assistant Manager had told her not to get too friendly with the grievant.

At this stage of the proceedings the attorney for the Employer stipulated that the Assistant Manager in question was hard to get along with.

The grievant testified that she worked the cash register until October 20, 1981, then was placed on the a la carte line for approximately two weeks and then on the serving line for approximately two weeks just prior to her dismissal. The grievant further testified that she had had no consultations with anybody prior to her dismissal concerning the manner in which she was doing her work. The grievant further testified that all of her problems started on October 20, 1981, when the Assistant Manager had deliberately tried to cause her trouble and the grievant had insisted on getting her orders straightened out. The grievant testified that the counselor had heard the grievant giving her an order in re: the free lunch, and that that order was inconsistent with what the Assistant Manager had told the Manager.

The grievant further testified that immediately following she was evaluated on November 3, 1981, by Mrs. Robinson, and her evaluation was lowered. This evaluation was not the normal evaluation that is normally given each April of the school year. The grievant believed that this evaluation was made because she did on October 21, 1981, file a grievance concerning harassment that she was receiving and to reassign her back to her former position as cashier. The November 3, 1981, evaluation merely stated that she was instructed to keep track of the quantity of food on her line as just before the 5th lunch period she was out of sandwiches.

The grievant further testified that on November 30, 1981, she was again evaluated and because of her alleged belligerent attitude, she was terminated. The termination was apparently approved by the Assistant Principal and by Dr. Eastman.

Argument

It is uncontradicted from all of the evidence presented that the grievant was a very satisfactory employee until the incident of October 20, 1981. It is further uncontradicted from all of the evidence that the incident of October 20, 1981, was not the fault of grievant, and as the Assistant Principal testified, this incident was not taken into consideration in the termination. It is further obvious from the evidence presented that when the grievant filed a grievance concerning harassment by the Assistant Manager on

October 21, 1981, the Manager was faced with a serious problem in her department, either she had to choose between her Assistant Manager or the grievant. Mrs. Robinson apparently chose to terminate the grievant, rather than incur the wrath of the Assistant Manager. Further, Mrs. Robinson was afraid at that time that if the grievance on harassment filed on October 21, 1981, progressed through to higher officials, she probably would bring too much attention to the manner in which she was conducting her position as a supervisor. Apparently, Mrs. Robinson consulted with Dr. Eastman and he suggested special evaluations and termination to avoid further publication of the fact that the Assistant Manager was hard to get along with.

It is elementary in employee relations that progressive discipline be given in an effort to rehabilitate a good employee who is starting to go downhill. Progressive discipline is not only proper, but it is just good plain common sense. No evidence was presented by any of the witnesses that progressive discipline was even considered. In fact, the evidence indicated that this termination even bypassed the normal channels and was not processed by the Personnel Department. The unusual handling of this termination would further indicate that the Personnel Department may have tried to resolve this grievance and might even have granted same had normal procedures been used.

Just cause for any dismissal cannot be sustained on the November 3, 1981 evaluation concerning being out of sandwiches on the 5th lunch period. Particularly, when the employee had just been transferred to a new responsibility, without having any special instructions in her duties and responsibilities. As to the allegations contained in the November 3, 1981 evaluation, the evidence presented by the fellow workers indicated just the opposite of this evaluation. As to the termination evaluation on November 30, 1981, this too occurred after a change in assignments without specific instructions in the new responsibilities. This newest evaluation did indicate that she no longer had a belligerent attitude. Again no attempt was made to counsel employee, to suggest ways in which she could satisfy the requirements of the supervisor, nor any type of warning concerning future action. Dismissal was recommended.

It is apparent from all of the evidence presented that the Supervisor found herself between a rock and a hard place and determined to terminate the grievant, rather than try to solve the real question before her, which was the attitude of the Assistant Manager.

Conclusion

The grievant submits that there is no just cause for this termination, that there is no just cause for any type of disciplinary action against the grievant, and that the grievant should be reinstated with all back benefits lost.

Respectfully submitted,

Charles S. Brown, Jr.
BROWN AND BROWN
116 North Main Street
New Castle, Indiana 47362
(317) 529-1305

Attorney for the Grievant

Opinion of the Arbitrator

To resolve the issues in this matter, the arbitrator is called upon to make four determinations: (1) whether the dispute is arbitrable, (2) whether cause for discharge existed, (3) whether the Grievant's contractual rights were violated, and (4) whether the discipline was arbitrary, capricious, disparate, or discriminatory.

1. Arbitrability

Employer contends, in effect, that the Grievant's failure to specify the exact contractual clause that was allegedly violated, not to mention the manner in which Employer's action violated said clause, renders the complaint non-arbitrable. Employer's position is clearly untenable. It would require a degree of legal training and familiarity with labor relations law not commonly found among employees. Thus, the requirement would effectively disfranchise most employees of their contractual rights.

Employer mistakenly equates its standard management rights clause to a clause excluding specific issues from arbitration; the two are not the same. The standard management rights clause reserving to the employer the exclusive right to make certain decisions does not automatically preclude arbitration of employee challenges of these decisions. As long as the contract deals with the issue in dispute, (i.e., contains language arguably covering the issue), defines grievance as a difference over contract interpretation or applications, and *does not* specifically, clearly, and unambiguously prohibit arbitration of the issue, the matter is arbitrable. In short, implied exclusions by way of standard management rights clauses are not sufficient, standing alone, to render otherwise arbitrable disputes non-arbitrable. Thus, Employer's argument that its management rights provisions—Section II of the *Policy Booklet*—preclude arbitration of the dispute before the Arbitrator is without merit.

Finally, the definition of grievance contained in Section IV of the *Policy Booklet*, namely:

> GENERAL—A grievance shall be defined as a difference between the administration and an employee involving an *alleged* violation, misinterpretation or misapplication of the policies, rules, or regulations contained in this employee policy booklet. (Emphasis added)

also supports the arbitrability of the dispute currently before the arbitrator. The use of the word "alleged" in the foregoing definition of grievance subjects any employer action which the employees *believe* violated the *Policy Booklet* to the grievance-arbitration procedure. The implication is that, if the parties do not themselves resolve the difference, final resolution will be made by the arbitrator—hence, the arbitrability of a wide range of disputes.

It should also be noted in passing that, contrary to Employer's claim, the Grievant does *allege* a specific violation of the *Policy Booklet*—that Employer violated its right to "suspend or discharge its employees in accord with applicable law." Granted, the manner of the alleged violation is not spelled out, but, in "protesting my discharge at Snider High School," the Grievant is alleging a violation of Section II of the *Policy Booklet*. Short of arguing the grievance in detail on the Official Grievance Form, this Arbitrator cannot see the way in which the grievant could have a much greater degree of specificity.

2. Cause for Discharge

It is incumbent upon Employer to establish, *prima facie*, the cause for discharge. The quantum of proof generally required in discharge cases to establish, *prima facie*, cause is clear and convincing evidence. The latter standard will be used to resolve the matter at hand.

Employer argues that, since non-certified employees of school systems only enjoy those rights which have been wrested from management in collective bargaining and since, in the case before the Arbitrator, the employees did not successfully negotiate a just cause limitation upon management's exclusive right to discharge, "an employee has no right to continued employment and may be terminated for cause or without any cause at all." While Employer's position concerning the origin of employer rights (i.e., concerning the so-called "reserved rights doctrine") is *generally valid*, it is flawed in the present case—on several counts, namely:

1. An employer may not use "reserved rights" to destroy other rights specified in the contract. Employer's position concerning discharge without showing cause threatens and otherwise compromises the employee rights specified in Appendix B of the *Policy Booklet*—particularly employee rights stemming from seniority. As Arbitrator Donnelly observed:

   > If the Company can discharge without cause, it can lay off without cause. It can recall, transfer, or promote in violation of the seniority provisions simply by invoking its claimed right to discharge. Thus, to interpret the Agreement in accord with the claim of the Company would reduce to a nullity the fundamental provision of a labor-management agreement—the security of a worker in his job.[1]

   Modern collective bargaining agreements, therefore, by nature, imply a just cause limitation upon the employer's right to discipline and discharge.[2]

2. Although Section II #4 of the Policy Booklet does not contain an explicit just cause limitation upon Employer's right to discipline and discharge, one may reasonably be inferred from the *Work Rules for Classified Employees* (i.e., Joint Exhibit #3) which must be read in conjunction with Section II #4. The *Work Rules for Classified Employees* reads, in part, as follows:

   > The following is a list of actions which may lead to disciplinary action, including suspension with or without pay or termination of employment, for those employees found to have committed them.

   The above statement, not to mention the list of work rules itself, places a just cause limitation upon Employer's right to discipline. The language utilized implies that all infractions of rules are not equally serious, that the gravity of a rule infraction depends upon the circumstances, that punishment should fit the crime, and discipline the infraction—in short, just cause. Arbitrators have not hesitated under these circumstances to accord to implied just cause limitations a weight equal to that accorded explicit just cause limitations.[3]

3. Finally, a strong argument can be made that the employment relationship involves a *quid pro quo* exchange of obligations; an employee agrees to perform specified duties in exchange for, among other things, an agreement from the employer that the employee will not be terminated without cause.

Employer's argument that there was not a just cause limitation upon its right to discipline and discharge is, therefore, without merit.

Although its position concerning the existence of a just cause limitation in the contract is not tenable, Employer does present a convincing and compelling case that the Grievant, M, was discharged for cause—that is, the failure to carry out her assigned job responsibilities in a satisfactory manner. The evidence is clear and convincing on the point—most importantly, Grievant's two unsatisfactory job evaluations of 11/3/81 and 11/30/81 as supported by the arbitration hearing testimonies of Laura Robinson, Grievant's immediate supervisor, Arlene Zumbrun, Assistant Principle of Snider High School, and Bev Leach and Eve Lanie, two of Grievant's cafeteria co-workers—all of whom had nothing to gain from the testimony given. On the other hand, evidence offered by Grievant's witnesses either did not refute Employer's evidence that *overall* job performance was unsatisfactory (i.e., testimonies of Amber Wyatt and Vera Woodward), did not speak well of Grievant's ability to take directions while operating the cash register (e.g., testimony of Anita Evans) or, in the case of the Grievant's own testimony, was self-serving. Employer has therefore established in clear and convincing fashion just cause for discharge.

3. Violation of Grievant's Contractual Rights—Right to Due Process

Union contends that the Grievant, M, was denied due process (i.e., progressive discipline) when Employer violated contractually guaranteed procedural requirements for discipline and discharge. Specifically, Union contends Employer violated Section III-A of the Policy Booklet, which states:

> Employees shall have the right to discuss with the school employer, individually *or through their representatives*, for purposes of establishing, *maintaining*, or improving wages and *related fringes* and policy. (Emphasis added)

when it refused the Grievant permission to have a union representative present for the discussion of the job evaluation conducted on November 3, 1981 (i.e., Employer Exhibit #1). The burden of proving a contractual violation on the part of Employer rests with the Union. It will be presumed that Employer's actions were in conformity with contractual provisions until Union establishes, by a "preponderance of the evidence," the contrary.

The evidence is overwhelming that a contractual violation occurred. Employer's own witness, Laura Robinson, testified that she refused Grievant's request for union representation for purposes of discussing Grievant's job evaluation of November 3, 1981. Employer's own exhibit (i.e., Employer Exhibit #1) corroborates Laura Robinson's testimony. It reads, in part:

> M did not wish to talk with me without her union steward present. It is not policy to have a union representative present for an evaluation. I explained this to her and said if she didn't wish to go over the evaluation with me, I would simply give her her copy, which I did.

The Grievant was thus denied representation at the time of her job evaluation despite clear contractual language (i.e., Section III-A of the Policy Booklet) that employees shall have the "right to discuss with the school employer . . . through their representatives . . .

wages and related fringes." What employer "fringe" is more important than job security threatened by a poor evaluation?

The foregoing cannot be dismissed or brushed aside as a minor procedural error. On the contrary, it seriously impacts the merits of the case—the showing of just cause for discharge noted above. Employer strongly implies at two different points in its post-hearing brief, namely p. 6, where it states: "After that evaluation, she failed to improve, and she received a second unsatisfactory evaluation on November 30, 1981, and was discharged," and p. 8, where it states:

> She was warned in the first evaluation (Board Exhibit #1). That evaluation was just about as negative as an evaluation can be. When she failed to improve, she was given the second evaluation and terminated. That is what she should have expected.

that:

(1) it took an even-handed approach in applying progressive discipline in the discharge case of M,
(2) the reason for Grievant's ultimate discharge was her failure to improve her job performance (i.e., to take corrective measures) following the unsatisfactory job evaluation of November 3, 1981, and
(3) had improvement taken place (i.e., had corrective measures been undertaken), the disputed disciplinary action (i.e., discharge) would not have been assessed on November 30, 1981.

Yet, Grievant was not permitted, through representation, to probe the seriousness and possible consequences of the poor job evaluation of November 3, 1981. A strong argument can be made, therefore, that Employer's contract violation precluded appropriate corrective action from being taken which would have prevented discharge. Given her satisfactory employment record up until September 1981 (Union Exhibit #1) and the language of the contract, Grievant deserved better treatment than she was accorded. Thus, Employer's contract violation and procedural error seriously taint (i.e., undermine) the propriety of the discharge—just cause established above—thereby warranting arbitral disturbance of the penalty imposed.

4. Disparate/Discriminatory Treatment

Union argues that the Grievant's disciplinary proceeding was handled in a different fashion than those of other disciplined employees, that the manner in which it was handled constituted an abuse of Employer discretion, and that, consequently, Employer's action was arbitrary, capricious, and discriminatory in nature. The burden of proof that Employer acted in a discriminatory or disparate fashion toward the Grievant rests with the party making the statement—the Union. The presumption that Employer's action was proper will stand until Union establishes, by a "preponderance of the evidence," that it was not. To proceed in contrary fashion would unduly burden the Employer by encouraging all employees who are disciplined to charge discrimination/disparate treatment and challenge the Company to disprove it.

In the present case before the arbitrator, Union did not establish, by a "preponderance of the evidence," that Employer's action was discriminatory or otherwise arbitrary—*did not* establish unlike treatment in like circumstances. What the Union did indicate was that some of the managerial personnel involved in the decision-making may have been different from those involved in preceding and subsequent discipline cases—evidence which, in itself, says nothing about discriminatory or disparate treatment.

Award

Based on the stipulations of the Parties, the evidence, the facts, and the circumstances of this case, the following award is made:

(1) The grievance of M is found to be arbitrable and properly before the arbitrator. Employer's motion to dismiss the grievance on grounds that it is not arbitrable is denied.
(2) The grievance of M is found to be meritorious in light of the serious procedural impropriety (i.e., contract violation) that marked Employer's termination action. Employer's motion to uphold termination and dismiss the grievance is denied.
(3) Given the incontrovertible evidence the Grievant failed to satisfactorily execute her job responsibilities during the three-month period, September through November, 1981, the requested remedy of *reinstatement with back pay is denied.* Instead, Fort Wayne Community Schools is *ordered to reinstate M without back pay* upon receipt of this award.

Clarence R. Deitsch
March 15, 1982
Muncie, Indiana

NOTES

1. Arbitrator Donnelly, *Atwater Manufacturing Company* 13 LA 747, 749.
2. For example, see: Arbitrator Oppenheim in 52 LA 1164, 1166–1167; Eaton in 51 LA 331, 331–333; Volz in 50 LA 1217, 1219; Jones in 48 LA 240, 241–242.
3. For example, see: Arbitrator Seidenberg in 52 LA 547, 551–552; Sherman in 48 LA 1209, 1212; Merrill in 46 LA 1044, 1046–1047.

Annotated Bibliography

This bibliography is not intended to be a complete listing of sources on grievances and arbitration. The authors have selected those books, journals, and reporting services that, in their opinion, provide an adequate library for the practitioner or scholar interested in contract administration in the public sector.

BOOKS

Dilts, David A. and William J. Walsh. *Collective Bargaining and Impasse Resolution in the Public Sector*. New York: Quorum Books, 1988. A complete text on impasse resolution during collective bargaining in state and local government. This practical guide to contract negotiations is the foundation for a detailed analysis of mediation, fact-finding, interest arbitration, and experimental impasse resolution techniques.

Elkouri, Frank and Edna Asper Elkouri. *How Arbitration Works*, 4th ed. Washington, D.C.: Bureau of National Affairs, 1985. A comprehensive treatment of how arbitrators handle the various aspects of the issues placed before them. Focuses primarily on rights arbitration, but contains a chapter on interest arbitration. The hallmark of this book is its breadth of coverage.

Fairweather, Owen. *Practice and Procedure in Labor Arbitration*, 2d ed. Washington, D.C.: Bureau of National Affairs, 1983. Authoritative, in-depth, coverage of the procedural and evidential aspects of arbitration. Includes an accessible discussion of some of the complex points of law concerning enforcement, judicial review, and fair representation.

Hill, Marvin F. and Anthony V. Sinicropi. *Evidence in Arbitration*, 2d ed. Washington, D.C.: Bureau of National Affairs, 1987. Authoritative and complete analysis of evidence in labor arbitration. This book begins where Elkouri and Elkouri leave off and discusses such issues as credibility, burden of proof, and weight of evidence, among others.

Hill, Marvin F. and Anthony V. Sinicropi. *Management Rights: A Legal and Arbitral Analysis.* Washington, D.C.: Bureau of National Affairs, 1986. Complete analysis of managerial discretion and how arbitrators deal with management rights issues. Again, this book begins where Elkouri and Elkouri leave off.

Hill, Marvin F. and Anthony V. Sinicropi. *Remedies in Arbitration.* Washington, D.C.: Bureau of National Affairs, 1981. A complete analysis of remedies applied in both disciplinary and nondisciplinary matters. Authors review remedies for errors, punitive remedies, and the effects of external law on arbitral remedial authority.

Kagel, Sam. *Anatomy of a Labor Arbitration*, 2d ed. Washington, D.C.: Bureau of National Affairs, 1986. This classic is a basic "how to" book. The book focuses on the mechanics of a typical arbitration case from the investigatory stages to presentation.

Levin, Edward and Donald Grody. *Witnesses in Arbitration: Selection, Preparation, and Presentation.* Washington, D.C.: Bureau of National Affairs, 1987. How to screen, prepare, and handle witnesses in labor arbitration. Uses question-and-answer approach and draws numerous comparisons with courtroom rules.

Lewin, David, Peter Feuille, Thomas Kochan, and John T. Delaney. *Public Sector Labor Relations, Analysis and Readings*, 3d ed. Lexington, Mass.: Lexington Books, 1988. This text is a comprehensive book of readings and original analysis on a broad range of public sector collective bargaining topics.

Lewin, David and Richard Peterson. *The Modern Grievance Procedure in the United States.* New York: Quorum Books, 1988. A detailed analysis of grievance administration and the procedures used for grievance settlement in the United States. Concise and authoritative, the book presents a wealth of information as well as solid theoretical analysis of variations on grievance resolution mechanisms.

Nolan, Dennis R. *Labor Arbitration Law and Practice, In a Nut Shell.* St. Paul: West Publishing Company, 1981. As the name suggests, a brief sketch of the legal environment of arbitration, with highlights of the procedural and decision-making aspects of arbitration.

Prasow, Paul and Edward Peters. *Arbitration and Collective Bargaining: Conflict Resolution in Labor Relations*, 2d ed. New York: McGraw-Hill, 1983. Academic textbook presenting standard topics in labor relations, with special emphasis on dispute resolution. Excellent; a classic reference in the field.

Volz, Marlin M. and Edward P. Goggin, eds. *1985–87 Supplement to How Arbitration Works.* Washington, D.C.: Bureau of National Affairs, 1988. An update of the work found in the Elkouris' *How Arbitration Works*, 4th ed. The supplement focuses on recent cases, extends the original work, and is well worth having.

Zack, Arnold. *Understanding Grievance Arbitration in the Public Sector.* Washington, D.C.: U.S. Department of Labor, 1975. Brief practitioners' guide to public sector grievance arbitration. This paperback is well written, easily understood, and presents the basics.

PERIODICALS

Arbitration Journal. New York: American Arbitration Association. Written for the practitioner. Contains articles concerning labor arbitration but also other forms of arbitration, such as construction and international disputes.

Employee Rights and Responsibilities Journal. Morgantown, W.V.: Council for Employee Rights and Responsibilities. Interdisciplinary journal focusing on a broad range of topics concerning employment relations, including labor-management relations and legal issues.

Journal of Collective Negotiations in the Public Sector. Massapequa, N.Y.: Baywood Publishing. Focuses on the public sector. Has a balanced approach primarily presenting results of original research, but most is readily understandable to the practitioner. Probably the single best source on state and local collective bargaining issues. A few articles are methodologically rigorous.

Journal of Conflict Resolution. New York: Sage Publications. Academic journal dealing with a wide range of conflict resolution topics, including labor-management relations. Also includes articles on international affairs and other dispute resolution forums. Some articles are methodologically rigorous.

Journal of Labor Research. Fairfax, Va.: George Mason University. Newest of the big three academic journals of industrial and labor relations. Primary focus is labor unions and their role in society. Most articles are accessible to the practitioner.

Industrial and Labor Relations Review. Ithaca, N.Y.: Cornell University. Oldest of the big three academic journals. Broad coverage of labor relations topics. Heavily oriented toward methodological rigor and of limited value to the practitioner.

Industrial Relations. Berkeley, Calif.: University of California. Another of the big three academic journals. Primary focus is academic research, primarily the behavioral aspects of collective bargaining. Much of the research is accessible to the practitioner.

Labor Law Journal. Chicago, Ill.: Commerce Clearing House. Written primarily for the practitioner; contains current articles on arbitration as well as other aspects of labor law.

CASE REPORTING SERVICES

Labor Arbitration Reports. Washington, D.C.: Bureau of National Affairs. Contains the complete and current texts of selected arbitrators' awards.

Labor Arbitration Awards. Chicago, Ill.: Commerce Clearing House. Contains the complete and current texts of selected arbitrators' awards.

Labor Relations Press. Port Washington, Pa.: Labor Relations Press. Provides listings of arbitrators' awards; complete texts of awards available for a page charge.

Summary of Labor Arbitration Awards. New York: American Arbitration Association. Contains brief summaries of arbitrators' awards, but allows the reader to order, for a small fee, the complete text of an award. AAA publishes specialized case reporting for the public sector and schools.

Index

ABOUT THE AUTHORS

CLARENCE R. DEITSCH is Professor of Economics at Ball State University and an active arbitrator. He is the author or co-author of over thirty articles appearing in such publications as *The Journal of Labor Research* and *The Arbitration Journal*, and is also the author of three other books on labor management relations topics.

DAVID A. DILTS is Professor of Business and Economics at Indiana University, Fort Wayne. His articles have appeared in *Management Science* and *The Journal of Labor Research*, and his previous books include *Collective Bargaining and Impasse Resolution in the Public Sector* (Quorum, 1988).